BOARD GAMES
~ THAT TELL ~
STORIES
IGNACY TRZEWICZEK

IGNACY TRZEWICZEK

BOARD GAMES
~THAT TELL~
STORIES
IGNACY TRZEWICZEK

Portal Games

Ignacy Trzewiczek

Ignacy
Trzewiczek

IGNACY
TRZEWICZEK

IGNACY TRZEWICZEK

IGNACY TRZEWICZEK

Ignacy
Trzewiczek

IGNACY
TRZEWICZEK

So, here I am. A designer. A publisher. And right now, the author of the book I dreamed of.

IGNACY TRZEWICZEK

Ignacy was born on September 23, 1976. Married to Merry and a father of two, he lives in Bojszów, a village near Gliwice, Poland. In 1999 he founded the RPG magazine 'Portal' and a company to publish it, becoming a publisher and soon after a designer. Ignacy is a great football (soccer) fan.

 Follow me on twitter: @trzewik
Subscribe to: http://boardgamesthattellstories.wordpress.com/

IGNACY'S DESIGNS AND CO-DESIGNS

Role Playing Games
Władca Zimy (2001), an unofficial supplement for Warhammer Fantasy Roleplay
Neuroshima RPG (2002) and its supplements (2003-2010), a postapocalyptic RPG
Monastyr (2004) and its supplements (2004-2010), a dark fantasy RPG
Play Smart (2010), *Play Tricky* (2011) - RPG Game Master's almanacs

Board Games
Machina (The Machine) (2002)
Gody (Courtship) (2003)
Zombiaki (Zombies) (2003)
Machina 2: Reloaded (2006)
Władcy Smoków (Dragon Lords) (2007)
Witchcraft (2008)
Stronghold (2009)
Prêt-à-Porter (2010)
51st State (2010)
Stronghold: Undead (2010)
Zombiaki 2: Attack on Moscow (2010)
New Era (2011)
Winter (2012)
Convoy (2012)
Robinson Crusoe: Adventure on the Cursed Island (2012)
Voyage of the Beagle (2013)

Coming in 2014
Imperial Settlers
The Witcher Adventure Game
That's NOT all, folks!

THANKS!

Thank you, Morano and Night.
Thank you Eric, Michiel, Rafał and Angus.
Thank you, the stretch goal texts' authors.
And thank you, all the backers of this project on kickstarter.com.
You made my dream come true.

INTRODUCTION

by Angus Abranson

Portal Publishing first came to my attention in 2001 when Hogshead Publishing published an English language edition of their fantastic *De Profundis* – a Lovecraftian letter writing game which was part of Hogshead's 'New Style' series of play. *De Profundis*, along with several other of Hogshead's 'New Style' games such as *The Extraordinary Adventures of Baron Munchausen*, partially inspired designers, creators and publishers to try new techniques and ideas which eventually led to the Indie Press boom we saw in the 2000's, which has just continued to grow.

Portal didn't stop with *De Profundis* of course, they carried on publishing roleplaying games from the 'New Style' likes of *Frankenstein Factoria* to the more mainstream *Neuroshima* and *Monastyr*. James Wallis closed Hogshead down towards the end of 2002 and that also meant the English language version of *De Profundis* slipping out of print.

At the time I was in a bit of a 'perfect storm'. Hogshead had been publishing *SLA Industries* – a grim dystopian science fiction RPG which was owned by Nightfall Games, of which I was one of the owners. I was also managing a large games retailer in London and had seen the success of *De Profundis* and the growing rise in interest of the smaller 'indie' games scene and different non-traditional ways of approaching roleplaying. Plus I was just starting to form a new publishing company called Cubicle 7 Entertainment which I wanted to use to publish cool and interesting games created by ourselves as well as other designers and small studios to help them get a wider audience.

I got Ignacy's details off James and emailed him in the early months of 2003 about the possibility of reprinting an English *De Profundis*. Ignacy was interested but, at the time I believe there were discussions in Poland about expanding it into a new edition, so he wasn't keen on having a direct reprint at the time – but then he started talking to me about the games that both he and his company produced...

I finally managed to meet Ignacy in person at Spiel in Essen in, I believe, October 2003. Certainly I have emails and manuscripts from the end of 2003 that we traded so I believe it was that year that Ignacy and I sat down at his booth and spoke about games and he showed me his first card game, *Zombiaki*, which was a great little 2-player game. Little did either of us know that in the following years Ignacy and Portal Publishing would grow to become one of the 'must see' companies exhibiting at Spiel each year with a string of successful and really interesting board games translated and published in a variety of languages.

It was great to see both Portal, and Ignacy, achieve success on the international stage. The correspondence we've had over the last 10+ years on games, game design, the differences in markets and player attitudes in different countries and cultures, has been immensely interesting and educational. I've often followed his blog posts and am pleased that he has finally decided to compile many of those into this volume.

I hope you find his thoughts and ideas as interesting and insightful as I have, and I certainly look forward to many more years of friendship and innovation to come.

Angus Abranson
Swindon, United Kingdom, October 2013

BOARD GAMES
~THAT TELL~
STORIES
IGNACY TRZEWICZEK

IGNACY TRZEWICZEK

YOU GOT TO HAVE GUTS...

Last weekend in Bulgaria the final of The Volleyball World League took place. The Polish team beat the US team 3:0. It was nice, thank you very much Americans!

Anyway, when I was watching the match I realized that you can learn quite a bit as a designer when you take a closer look at volleyball.

You know, for almost my whole life the rules of scoring in volleyball were as follows: when you serve and win the point, you score. When your opponent serves and you win the point, you don't score, you just have the right to serve. Then if your attack is successful, you score. However, if your opponent manages to win the point, he only has the right to serve...

The official volleyball federation was founded in 1947. For 50 years people played according to the rules described above. If you serve, and I win, I don't get a point. I only get the right to serve. So now I serve, but this time you win, so you don't score, but now you can serve... And it goes on like that for two hours. The score? 0:0.

Watching volleyball was kinda boring for over 50 years.

And then somebody finally figured it out. This game is broken, he said. We have to change the rules. You need to score after every successful attack, no matter who served.

It's not easy to change the rules of a game that has been played competitively for over 50 years. A game that was played in world championships, during Olympics, a game with official leagues all over the world.

But the Federation of Volleyball had the balls to make the change.

They had the guts to say: 'Our game sucks. We can make it better.' And they changed the rules. It was 1998, 51 years after the federation had been founded, and they had the guts to remove the one rule that was making volleyball boring.

Volleyball has become much more simple. It is fast, and extremely engaging. It is a great sport now.

***

This is a nightmare for a designer. You design a game. You test the game, you play a lot, you get used to this rule. Finally you're stuck with it. But you didn't ask yourself an important question:

'Does my game really need this rule?'

It is hard to ask this question. There is a risk you will get a negative answer. You would need to delete this rule. The rule you got used to. The rule you liked. This very rule...

So you're stuck with it. Your game is filled with rules that don't add anything to the gameplay. They don't make the game better. They don't give more choices. They don't elicit more emotions. They just exist. They just exist because you got used to them after all those test games.

All those rules could be removed if you had the guts to ask the question.

***

I am a young designer. Yes, I was lucky to make some – I believe good - games like *Stronghold* or *The New Era*, but this is just the beginning. I am aware of that. I am still in the primary school of designing. I am learning every single day. I have flaws that I need to rid myself of. I know that.

One of my flaws is putting too many rules into my games. I have difficulties with designing simple games. It's hard for me to delete rules, to ask myself the question: 'Does my game really need this rule?'

But I am working hard on this issue. I am trying to improve. I am aware of the problem and I believe this is a good start. I see the problem. This is always a good first step.

In the last months I have been working damn hard on *Robinson Crusoe*. The game is ready. Works really well. I am proud of it and I can't wait for you guys to see it. But it's not going to print yet. I still have a few weeks left.

During these weeks I will ask myself the question.

In 1998 the volleyball federation showed that they have guts. Now it is my time to act.

SCANIA, I SEE A MARKET FOR YOU HERE!

You board gamers know that vacation is a great time. This is the moment when we can finally play all those great games we have been buying and collecting for the whole year!

Is it raining all day? Everybody on vacation is pissed off, except us, board gamers! Rain, this is great! You will have to stay in your hotel room, and now you will finally have time to open that copy of *Arkham Horror* (with all its expansions?!) you bought a decade ago and play it for 24 hours straight!

Is it cold? Don't go sightseeing, it sucks and you can catch a cold! Stay in your hotel room, open your suitcase and reveal its contents: *Twilight Imperium, third edition.* Oh yes, I wish it would stay cold for two whole weeks. No problem at all.

Nice weather? OK, let it be nice weather. I am not a big fan of nice weather, but what the hell, I am prepared! I can go to the beach. I can go to the beach with *Cash & Guns, Tichu, Hystericoach* and we will have lots of fun.

You have brought your kids? Give them *Talisman* and you won't need to look after them for the next 6 hours. Giving them *Talisman* is like hiring a nanny, only better, because it can handle up to 6 kids! What nanny can beat this?!

You are with friends who don't know board games yet? Get *Ticket to Ride* to the table and watch how their eyes open with excitement and new born passion. This is a huge moment. It is worth playing *Ticket to Ride* for the 328th time in your life.

You are with die hard geeks? Lucky bastard, make it a *Neuroshima Hex* vacation! Start a league, play every day, keeping track of results, with a league table and a final prize.

Oh yes. Board games are the answer to all vacation situations.

That's why I have everything with me here on vacation. *Settlers of Catan* to play with the kids. *Twilight Struggle* to play with my wife. *Brawl* to play a tournament with my friend Widlak. *Neuroshima Hex* so our kids can play a tournament. The prototypes of *Robinson* and *Winter* so I can test it with my friends. Yes, vacations and games work very well together.

But... There is one small question I have to ask.

How the hell am I supposed to get all these games into my car?! Where to put clothes and all other necessities?! I need a truck!

Scania, I see a huge market for you here. I will need to rent a truck for two weeks. And my fellow geeks too. What are the prices? Any discount for BGG members?

SCANIA,
I SEE A MARKET FOR YOU HERE!

Lloyd

otakar.z

'How the hell am I supposed to pack all these games into my car?!'.
My photo (first) and the received feedback by and KAS (otakar.z's photo).

IGNACY TRZEWICZEK

YES, YOU CAN

We are preparing the final files to print *Robinson Crusoe*. We are ordering wooden cubes, we are ordering cards, we are preparing lots of different tokens. We are doing all that stuff that I really really hate. One mistake and man, you are in serious trouble. *Robinson* is a huge, epic game. It reminds me of *Stronghold*. It reminds me of August 2009...

***

In August 2009, when we were finishing the work on *Stronghold*, every single day I was wondering what mistake we would make. I wasn't wondering if we would make a mistake. I was wondering what mistake it would be. Oh yes, I was sure that we would botch something up. Nearly 150 tokens, nearly 100 cards, a 60 page long rulebook in 3 languages, more than 300 wooden pieces. It was a big production with an 'FFG' impetus. It was like a ride on a rollercoaster. It was fast, exciting and it had to end badly. In August 2009 I had no doubts about that.

We were not FFG. Portal consisted of three guys. Three guys making the biggest game in their lives. Three guys scared as hell. Three guys who wanted to make a good worldwide impression. Three guys who tried to create an 'FFG production'.

We had no marketing department and yet we were on the #1 place on BGG's The Hotness list for many weeks before Essen. We had no budget for advertisement and yet we had a movie trailer presenting *Stronghold*. We had no copywriters and yet with our Game Design Journal series we were one of the most discussed games before the Essen fair.

The production of *Stronghold* exceeded our possibilities. Not just exceeded, but greatly exceeded what we considered possible. The magnitude of the undertaking left us breathless. We were doing our best. And every day we were motivating each other to try harder. It was the time of our lives. Our biggest game.

You gamers saw the cover and the board of *Stronghold*, you read the GDJ stuff, you watched the movie trailer, you were participating in this whole hype and buzz, and then, after Essen, you were nominating us for the International Gamer Award or the Golden Geek, but did you know that this whole project was accomplished by just 3 friends?

Portal's production department? The entire department – Michał Oracz.

The testing team? Oh, sure! A huge team! Rafał Szyma and Ignacy Trzewiczek (and a bunch of our closest friends).

The marketing department? His Majesty the Storyteller, Ignacy Trzewiczek.

The artwork director? Michał Oracz, once again.

The game development team? A one man team – Ignacy Trzewiczek, again.

The movie trailer? Michał Oracz.

The Essen stand designer? Michał Oracz.

And so forth...

Yes, it was crazy, but we did it. There were no mistakes in *Stronghold*. We created one of the most talked about and well respected games of 2009. It was awesome.

***

Today Portal is twice as big. We have grown, but still, we are nothing but a bunch of friends doing their best to bring you the best games possible. This year we will give you *Robinson Crusoe*. This year again

A photo from the old times, when there were only three of us in Portal Games.
From the left: Michał Oracz and Rafał Szyma, 2007.

we will have to exceed our possibilities. This year again we will do everything in our power to reach the dizzy heights of FFG and other great publishers.

Have dreams. Have courage to follow these dreams. Create your games. You don't need to have a big budget. You don't need to have a crew of 20 people. You don't need anything except passion and a will to fight. Fight for your success. It is at your fingertips.

POLAND HAS GAMERS

I may be wrong in today's post. I may not have the right perspective. But what the hell, this is my blog and I will write here what I feel. And I truly believe that here in Poland we did a great job, enriching the gaming hobby in the past 5 years.

***

From my perspective it all started in 2007, when Portal presented *Neuroshima Hex* in Essen. I remember the words that Greg J. Schloesser spoke that year. They were: 'I honestly don't know much – OK, anything – about the gaming scene in Poland, but if *Neuroshima Hex* is any indication I am impressed.'

At the time, Poland was a blank spot on the board game map. No gamer knew anything about Poland or Polish games. With *Neuroshima Hex* we made a grand entrance.

Today, *Neuroshima Hex* is a game known worldwide, ranked #138 on BGG, with thousands of copies in gamers' collections, six new armies published as expansions, and more than 20 fan armies published as PDF files. There are US, French, Spanish, Dutch, Italian and of course Polish editions. New editions are in progress. It is fantastic what *Neuroshima Hex* has achieved.

Two years later, in 2009, Portal published *Stronghold*, another great epic game that was widely discussed. *Stronghold* was nominated for the International Gamers Award, for the Golden Geek, for the Game of the Year in Poland and then was licensed and published worldwide by Valley Games. Without false modesty I do believe that designing *Stronghold* was important for many players. No such game existed before *Stronghold*.

We did a bunch of other games, like *51st State* or *Pret-a-Porter*, but Poland is not only Portal...

***

In 2010, a Polish company – Rebel.pl – published *K2*, a great family game about climbing the second-highest mountain on Earth. It is a great board game, with easy rules and engaging gameplay. It was designed by my friend, Adam Kałuża, who lives 20 miles away from me. This year Adam and his *K2* were nominated for the Kennerspiel des Jahres. It is a huge success. Many players have since decided to try *K2* and I believe they will love it, they will try to climb and risk a hard path or an easy one, and will have to decide when to attack the mountain and when to rest... Simple rules, great game play. I do believe that Adam, by designing *K2*, has added another small gem to our hobby...

***

And since we're talking about gems... There is a guy called Edrache, a friend of mine from Poznan, who in March 2010 started a tremendous project called Minimalistic posters. His geek list on BGG gathered 886 'thumbs up' and this is not a surprise. It is great stuff. He decided to design posters for different board games. His work was so great that Hans im Glück contacted Edrache and asked him to design 12 posters for their games. They published them in a calendar.

I was happy to have my games 'postered' by Edrache. The poster of *Stronghold* is hanging in a passe-partout in my room. I love it. I have the pleasure to know Edrache and to be able to game with him.

These 886 'thumbs' up are quite a few. Edrache introduced to our hobby something that is interesting and new, something that enriched our hobby.

***

In addition to all this, we have two war gamers who have brought something really special to the board game scene during the last few years. Robert Żak designed *Strike of the Eagle*, which was at first published in Poland and then licensed and published by Academy Games. I haven't played it myself yet, but the reviews are quite clear – this is a great war game. *Conflict of Heroes: Price of Honour – Poland 1939* is a similar example, co-designed by Michał Ozon and published by Academy Games. Once again I haven't played it yet, but it is on my short list to play, already on my shelf, waiting for a free evening. These are great games from Polish designers. I am eager to play them.

***

And last but not least, my close friend Pancho. In 2000 when I was publishing an RPG magazine, Pancho was one of the writers and he wrote really great stuff for the Warhammer RPG. When in 2010, ten years later, he told me that he had founded Big Daddy's Creations and asked me for the license for *Neuroshima Hex* for iOS, I just couldn't refuse. We had known each other for a decade.

But, I am a lucky bastard. Big Daddy's Creations created one of the greatest apps for iOS.

Neuroshima Hex is an example of one of the best adaptations of a board game for an electronic device. It was chosen as the second best board game app by IGN magazine. They won GameShark's iOS Game of the Year and were runners up in TouchGen's Best Card/ Board game category... They did an awesome job.

And then they did *Caylus*. And now they are doing *Eclipse*. This is a great crew from Poland.

***

In 3 weeks I will hold another edition of the board game convention in Gliwice. We will all meet up there.

Pancho will bring me some screen shots of *Stronghold* for the iPad. I am very excited about this release. I know they will do a wonderful job with this app.

Michał Ozon will bring a pre-production copy of *CLASH: Jihad vs. McWorld*. This is a rethemed version of *RRR*, a great abstract strategy game by Seiji Kanai that I brought from Essen two years ago and showed in Poland.

Adam Kałuża will show *The Cave*, his new game about exploring caves. This is his hobby and passion, and from what I hear, the game is as good as *K2*. Once again Adam has put his whole heart into his design.

I will show them my game, *Robinson Crusoe*, another take on an epic game with a strong theme. Like in 2009 with *Stronghold*, I once again spent almost the whole damn year working on it, and once again I believe I was able to put into *Robinson's* box my passion, imagination, and my heart. This is the great adventure co-op that I have been dreaming about for years.

We will all sit down together, share our ideas and designs, drink a beer or tea, and have fun. We are a nice bunch of gamers. This year we will have good stuff for you. Again.

DIE HARD MERRY

It was March 2011. I had finally completed the rules for *The New Era* expansion. I had new cards and I was ready to test it. I came back from work, ate supper, said good night to the kids and sat down at the table with my wife, Merry. I needed to see how those new rules worked. We played.

Merry was playing terribly. Chaos on the table. No good decisions. No strategy. It was terrible and yes, I really mean it. I was tired after work and I was disappointed with Merry's approach. At some point I just put my cards away and said: 'OK, we stop. You are playing like a moron. Thank you very much for such help!'

I was really disappointed that she didn't want to help me with testing.

Merry, however, didn't apologize. Her reaction was quite the opposite. She exploded. Yes, women do that.

'What?! I don't care?! I am only pretending to do my best?!' and it was just the beginning... 'I am playing here with you despite the fact that you didn't even care to explain the rules to me! I never played *51st State*, remember? I don't know what I am doing and I am desperately trying to understand these damn icons! I don't care?! Are you kidding me?!'

MR AND MRS TRZEWICZEK...

DYING HARD IN THE 51ST STATE

Essen 2012. From left: Gabor, Merry, Me, Hubert, Krisztina.

It always ends like that. The man is the one who is guilty. The man is to say 'sorry'. So I did. I took my cards back. I spent 20 minutes explaining the rules. We played again. Merry was playing well.

That night, Merry fell in love with *The New Era*.

***

Since then Merry has played countless games of *The New Era*. It could be more than 300 or even 500 games. I have no idea. She is playing all the time. She was testing it with me. Then, when *The New Era* was balanced and I was truly sick of it, she decided to find new players. And yes, she found them.

Are you going to visit Mr. and Mrs. Trzewiczek's house? You will play *The New Era*. Merry will explain the rules to you and make you play it.

Did you invite Mr. and Mrs. Trzewiczek to your home for a nice evening? Yes, Merry will 'by accident' have *The New Era* with her. She will explain the rules to you and make you play it.

Are you at a convention? Is Merry there too? She will hunt you down and teach you and play *The New Era* with you.

How about the board game club in Gliwice? Sure! Every single Monday she is there, playing *The New Era*...

***

'It has the same problem as *Race for the Galaxy*' she once told me. 'You've just developed your state, you have great cards built, you want to finally start scoring big points, but the game suddenly ends. You have 12 cards in RftG, or 33 points here and that's it. I want it to last longer.'

She looked at me. 'Could you...? Please?'

What is a man to do? Can he resist that look?

So I designed the *Winter* expansion.

***

I changed the pace of the game. Now it always lasts six turns. The game is much more strategic now. You plan your actions for all the following turns, you plan how to develop your state and you plan how many points you can make this time.

It is so much more satisfying. Or so much more frustrating when you see another player developing better, having a better plan, having their combos working more smoothly...

I removed the Leader cards and the Contact cards from the deck and added them to the Frozen City section – now it is no longer luck that decides whenever you have a Leader or not, it is up to you to take one.

I changed how production works – now it follows players' needs. In every turn it changes a little bit, so players get additional workers, additional cards or resources. It gives them great possibilities to create new combos and develop their state.

I played *Winter* many times and I am proud of it. I tested it for a few months and I believe it is great. But what is more, I saw Merry playing it hundreds of times with people. She is a die-hard fan of the *51st State* line and every time she played *Winter* I saw in her eyes that this is it, this is the expansion that fans are waiting for.

***

Writers sometimes, on the first page of their novel, write a dedication. Something like: 'For my beloved wife and kids' or 'For Jenny' or whatever.

Winter is not only dedicated to Merry. *Winter* was designed for her.

What can I say. You *51st State* fans are lucky bastards. You have a die-hard fan of the game living with me. She will be forcing me to design new cards for the next 20 years. Stay tuned.

WHY I NEEDED 3 YEARS
TO DISCOVER FROZEN CITY

In 2010 I designed *51st State*. I was proud as hell. It was a great game. I got great reviews, I got a few nominations for awards, I saw people playing it at many conventions and having a great time with it! I believed I had designed a perfect card game.

A year later I discovered that *51st State* is not a perfect game. A year later I designed direct interaction rules for *51st State* and that's how *The New Era* hit the market. With direct aggression *51st State* was just awesome. I once again believed I had designed a perfect card game.

A year later I discovered that *The New Era* is not a perfect game. I designed Frozen City and Production dice and that's how *Winter* hit the market. With Frozen City and Production dice *51st State* was just awesome. I believed I had finally designed a perfect card game...

***

Leaders

Leaders? Players who played *51st State* were complaining about them a lot. They are powerful and players who have them have a huge advantage. If you draw a Leader you are in a better position than your opponent. Many gamers complained. 'Leaders suck.', 'Leaders are unbalanced.', 'I play without Leaders!'

This is bad.

OK, let's take a moment to look at the problem. Are Leaders bad or is the distribution of the Leaders bad?

I take all the Contact cards and all the Leaders and put them aside. I put them on a special board called Frozen City. Every player can send a worker there whenever they want to have a new Leader. It is no longer a random draw. It is no longer a huge advantage. Everybody can have a Leader if he wants to. It is simple. It is obvious. Why didn't it work that way since the very beginning?

Why was I such a moron? Why did I need three years to discover this?

Production

It is the first round. You play the Merchants or the Mutants and you have – almost – no chance to attach a Location. Incorporating a new Location costs you two Iron, and at the beginning you don't have them. And no chance to get them. This is the first round and you know you will not be able to play a Location.

This is bad.

It is the last round, and you have six or seven Locations with the Action icon. Each of them needs a Worker, but you produce only 3 workers. Pity. You have been developing for an hour and now you are stuck. Half of your Locations will not work. It sucks.

This is bad.

In *51st State* production is constant – every single round you get 3 Workers and 1 Resource, but players' needs aren't constant. At the beginning they need iron to build Locations, then they need redevelopment tokens to change Locations, then they need a hell of a lot of Workers to take many Actions... Why not make the Production phase different for each round? Why not make the Production phase follow players' needs? Why not give them additional Iron at the beginning of the game and an additional worker at the end?

Why was I such a moron? Why did I need three years to discover this?

***

Every year, when I finish my new design I am 100% sure that it is a perfect game. I see no flaws. I see no points where it could be improved. I see it as a brilliant piece of work.

And year after year I learn something new. Every year I discover new stuff. Every year it turns out that I can do something better.

Today I am happy to announce – without false modesty – that *Winter* is a perfect card game.

But to be honest I have a hunch I may want to change this statement next year...

ARE YOU DESIGNING A GAME?
YOU BETTER HAVE VLAADA CHVATIL
IN YOUR TESTING GROUP!

The Czech Republic is close, so when a friend of mine recommended I visit a small Czech convention that took place a 3 hour drive from Gliwice, I didn't have to think too long. I took my wife, my daughter, I took *Robinson* and off we went! It was March or April, spring time, a great time for a nice weekend in the Czech Republic. This is a beautiful country from what I had heard!

Naturally, I didn't get to see much of the country. I didn't see the Czech Republic at all. I spent two days in a game room playing *Robinson Crusoe* and *Convoy*. But my wife said that the country is nice. She went for a small trip while I was playing...

Anyway, at some point when I was looking for new players to test *Robinson*, Vlaada Chvatil appeared in the room. One of the players asked him to join a test game. Vlaada looked at me, looked at *Robinson* and said: 'OK, let's play.' We began.

The game was tough. Players quickly got wounded. A few times they were very unlucky. Because of wounds they started to lose their character's skills (when you got a certain number of wounds, you would lose skills) and they started to despair. From the fourth turn onwards, Vlaada started to complain.

'We are going to die. We won't make it.'

I was in a good mood. The game was tough, they really needed to fight hard to survive on the island. I liked it. 'Stop complaining, fight. Do your best!' I told Vlaada.

Fifth round. They got another couple of wounds and again lost some of their character's skills. 'We are going to die next round,' said Vlaada.

'Stop doing that!' I said. 'You need to fight. You need to do your best. You need to survive. Think, try to find a solution.' I insisted.

'I am trying, but there is no solution. The game will finish us off next round.'

The other players weren't as demotivated as Vlaada, they saw chances, they tried. Vlaada gave up. He saw that the end was close.

Sixth round. Everyone died. Vlaada was right. They didn't make it.

***

'You should try harder.' I said.

'The game is poorly constructed. We had no chance.' Vlaada answered. He was thinking, looking at the cards, checking out the character boards, the dice. 'If I may suggest... Well, in my opinion you have a problem here, Ignacy. When players get wounded, they lose skills. This is bad,' he said.

'Are you kidding me? This is awesome! It's like Die Hard! You get wounded, you are bleeding, you have a broken leg, you feel pain all over your body, but you cannot give up, you need to fight!' That was exactly what I wanted. You get wounded, you lose skills, you have to try harder. 'It is like Bruce Willis, right? Wounded, bleeding, but still fighting back!'

'Ignacy, it isn't a movie. It is a board game,' Vlaada replied. I don't know if Vlaada likes Die Hard, but at that very moment, he didn't look like he was a big fan of John McClane.

'Vlaada, come on! It's like a Die Hard movie! You know, Bruce Willis in a torn shirt, lots of blood and fighting till the very end. Bruce Willis never gives up. That is the feeling I want to have here in *Robinson*. I want you bleeding, suffering, but still fighting to survive!'

'It's a board game. You are a designer. Not a director. Remember?'

***

'There is a serious problem here,' Vlaada had said. 'When you get a few wounds, and you reach a certain pain threshold, you lose your character's skills.'

'Yes, this represents you being tired, hurt, and then obviously you lose some abilities...'

'Put the story aside for a moment. Focus on the problem. You get wounds when you are in trouble. When the situation gets tough. You have a problem. But the game doesn't help. It knocks you down. You get a wound, you are in trouble, and on top of that the game takes away your skill. It is a double hit. You need tools to deal with the problems. But here, in *Robinson*, when you are in trouble, the game takes away your tools. You get the point?'

'Yep.' I may be a John McClane fan, but I am not an idiot... 'But if a character gets wounded and there are no consequences, getting a wound will not be a problem! I need players to be afraid of wounds!'

'It doesn't work. This mechanism is bad. You are in trouble. You get wounded and at the same moment you lose tools you need to get out of this shit. This is bad.'

He was right. He just took the whole 'wound mechanism' and threw it in the bin.

I hate when people are right.

I took my prototype and went back to my room.

No, I wasn't crying. True John McClane fans don't cry.

***

That night I didn't sleep well. To be honest I didn't sleep at all. Well, maybe two or three hours. Let's face it – if Vlaada Chvatil says that your game has a problem, you don't sleep. Right?

I spent a few hours rewriting the rules. Tried to find a solution. I wanted players to be afraid of getting wounds, but on the other hand I understood what Vlaada said about taking skills away. I changed the number of wounds required to take away a character's skills. I changed the skills, so when you lost them you wouldn't suffer as much. After a few hours I had a new set of skills, new pain thresholds and I was sure that now, when players got wounded, they would still have a chance to fight back. But still, getting wounds was bad, it was something that players would want to try to avoid.

I caught Vlaada at breakfast. 'Got a minute for me after breakfast?' I asked. 'Yes. Actually I wanted to talk with you. I was thinking about the game last night.'

I showed him my notes. I showed him how I had changed the pain thresholds and skills. I showed him how I had changed the wound rules and the consequences of wounds.

'Is it OK? Is this what you were talking about yesterday?' I asked.

'Well... It is a step in the right direction,' he said.

For all of you who don't get it – 'a step in the right direction' is a polite way of saying, 'Man, it sucks. Try harder.'

We talked about some other problems of *Robinson* for an hour. Then I packed *Robinson, Convoy,* my wife Merry and my daughter into the car, and we drove back to Poland. My entire game idea had been destroyed.

So here is my advice for all of you – think twice when you decide to take a prototype to the Czech Republic... - you might not have a prototype to bring back – it will be in the bin.

ARE YOU DESIGNING A GAME?
YOU BETTER HAVE VLAADA CHVATIL
IN YOUR TESTING GROUP! PART 2

I gave Merry the car keys. 'You drive. I work,' I said and I sat in the back seat. I had my *Robinson* prototype, shredded to pieces by Vlaada's comments. My beloved game was hurt and wounded. I had it right next to me. I also had lots of paper and a pencil. And in front of me I had a three hour trip to Poland.

I came to the Czech Republic to present my great game. I was going back with a game torn to pieces. Oh yes, I was pissed off.

So we are going home. Merry is driving. My daughter Lena is singing. I am working.

***

The problem – if a player gets wounded and as a consequence he loses a skill, he is unable to fight back and get out of trouble. But on the other hand, if a player gets wounded and there are no consequences, he is not afraid of getting wounds. And this sucks.

I look at the notes from last night, as well as the new rules I designed in the hotel room. 'It is a step in the right direction...,' Vlaada had said. 'The right direction'... I'll show you 'a step in the right direction'...

I tore it all to pieces. I don't want to hear about the right direction. I want: 'Ignacy, this is brilliant.'

Did I mention I may have been a little bit angry that day? Just a little.

I took a clean sheet of paper. I wrote: WOUNDS. CONSEQENCES. LOSING SKILLS.

I crossed out LOSING SKILLS.

WOUNDS. CONSEQUENCES. I needed a new approach. I needed a new point of view. Merry was driving. Lena was singing. I was working. And I was really pissed off.

***

The story is always the starting point. So I am sitting in the car and I am trying to imagine myself on the Island. I am trying to imagine that I am hurt. I am trying to imagine what is happening...

I am unhappy. I am scared. I am complaining. I want the rest of my mates to know that I got wounded so they know I won't be able to work as hard as I would like to. They are sad, demotivated, morale drops. I am complaining...

Morale drops. Hmm... Interesting. When a player gets a wound, morale drops. That is a new point of view, a new perspective.

There may be a morale track. It would show if players are motivated or not. It is one track for all. If one player gets a wound, it affects this track. The entire group suffers. The wounded player is complaining. He is crying. He is hurt and wounded. Team morale drops...

Oh, yes! I got it! Merry was driving. Lena was singing. I was pissed off, but I was getting close to the turning point – happiness here I come!

***

So what do we have here? The solution fits the story – which is always very important for me – if a player gets a wound, another wound and another one, at some point he starts to complain, demotivating the whole group. I can imagine it. It works with the theme, with a group of people on a deserted island. Team spirit. One for all, all for one.

What else do we have? If a player gets wounded, he doesn't lose any skills. I disconnect skills from wounds. You have skills till the very end, no matter how wounded you are. So when a player is in trouble, if he gets wounded, the game will not kick him down. He is still capable of fighting back.

What else? If a player gets wounded, the whole group suffers. This means that he doesn't want to get hurt because all players will be affected, but on the other hand, if he suffers, he can still take part in the action and he won't feel like he is out of the game. He will not have this bad feeling of no longer being part of the group. He is in the game till the very end.

The problem has been solved. Of course, at that moment in the car I had no idea how team morale would work, but that was just a small detail, right? The most important thing was shifting the penalty for getting wounded from one player to the entire group.

***

A few hours later I thought of something else. I can differentiate the characters. The explorer will have only one level of complaining. He can get six wounds in a row and he will not complain a single time. He is the hardened explorer. He has seen much worse. The cook? My dear, the cook is a moaning pig, he will complain after getting only three wounds, and then he will complain after getting two more, and then again, two wounds and again he is grumbling. You better have food for the cook, for if he goes hungry, he will get 2 wounds and will then wail like a slaughtered calf.

It is fun. In a very simple way it helps diversify characters. And it helps players feel at one with the character, feel the theme, feel the story. Some characters will cause morale to decrease often, others will not. Some are moaning pigs, others are tough like John McClane. This is simple and this is fun. This is good.

***

When we arrived home I was relaxed. My game had been repaired. Vlaada had pointed out the problems in my game, and I had managed to solve some of them during my way home and now my game was much better than 3 days before. When I got home I turned my laptop on, opened BGG and sent a geek mail to Vlaada. I was eager to once again thank him for his help. And very eager to tell him that the problem had already been solved.

Well, what can I say... I may not look like Bruce Willis. But when I am pissed of I get better. Just like John McClane...

THE LESSON

The game ended badly. One of the characters is dead. It is game over and it is game over in a bad way. They didn't stand a chance. They weren't even close. It wasn't a good game.

'You were unlucky. Too many bad events. It's an adventure game, sometimes you are lucky, sometimes you aren't...' I say. Vlaada is searching through the decks of cards. 'There are good and bad events in all of those decks?' he asks, pointing at the four decks of cards.

'Yep.'

'You can't have good events here, Ignacy,' he says.

Did I just hear him say what I think I heard him say?

'Are you kidding?! You just lost due to a lack of good events!'

'There cannot be good events in those decks. You have to get rid of them. You don't control the game at this moment. Ignacy, you – as an author – have to have control over your game.'

OK, I have to admit it – at that very moment I wasn't sure what he was talkin' about. Remove the good events? Why? Have control? How?!

I have, however, enough courage to ask. So I asked Vlaada to explain it to me. And he did.

'How many good and bad events did you design in that deck?' he asked, pointing at the Event deck.

'There are 40 good events and 60 bad events,' I answered. '*Robinson Crusoe: Adventure on the Cursed Island*. Statistically you will have 3 bad and 2 good events in the first part of the game, and then again 3 bad and 2 good events in the second part of the game.'

'You have to get rid of all good events. Ignacy, you don't control it. This is bad. You can't design a game that you don't control.'

Still no idea what he is talkin' about. And still enough courage to ask and learn.

'Vlaada, I don't get it.'

He took one of my sheets of paper and my pen. 'Look,' he said. 'During the set up you take five cards from this deck, right? You say that statistically there should be 3 bad and 2 good cards and that this is an average difficulty level, but...' and he started to write.

'There may be:

5 bad, 0 good

4 bad, 1 good

3 bad, 2 good

2 bad, 3 good

1 bad, 4...'

'I get it,' I said.

'You want the game to be difficult, you want the game to throw 3 bad events at the players, and you want the game to help them twice. That is your dream configuration. But math is cruel. There will be games like ours today, with 4 bad events and only 1 good. There will even be games with 0 bad and 5 good events. Players will play it, will have 5 good events, finish the game without the smallest effort and then they will write on BGG that the game is a piece of cake and boring, and that they don't recommend it.'

'You are right.'

'You need to control the game. Now it is a rollercoaster. You have no idea what will happen. It may be extremely easy. It may be extremely hard. Your intended configuration of 3/2 is only one of many possibilities. What about the others? You have to remove all the good events. You have to make it 5 bad events, 0 good events and then set the difficulty of the game.'

'Math sucks,' I said.

If I were Vlaada, I'd say that *Robinson* sucks, but Vlaada is a nice person. He didn't say that.

The conclusion? I had to take about 120 events from 5 different decks and throw them into the bin. I needed to take control over my game and to do so, I had to trash 40% of the cards I had designed over the last 4 months.

I did it. Without a blink of an eye.

The lesson? A few, actually.

Vlaada knows math.

Math is a bitch.

Game designers need to have the courage to throw their ideas into the bin and start from scratch.

That is what game design is all about – no mercy.

A NEW EXPANSION. FOR FREE.

It's the second half of August, we are in the town of Rowy, at a table right by the sea side. It's blissfully quiet, with only the sound of the waves crashing onto the beach while we play a game of *Citadels*. There's a mixed party here, two players from Gliwice, four from Warsaw. I have the Merchant in my hand, and I take two pieces of gold, plus a third one, and decide to build a Palace, when I suddenly hear it's not allowed...

'Excuse me?' I ask in surprise.

'You're not allowed to build after taking a third gold piece. You take gold after you've completed your actions,' is the answer.

'Yes I can.' I smile. 'I assure you, I can.'

We pick up the manual. I point at the relevant paragraph with my finger. We read it aloud, and all becomes quiet.

'Great. We've been playing it the wrong way for a year...'

A few moments pass, the Assassin kills the King. 'The crown goes to the dead king,' I point out, seeing that no one is willing to pass the crown. 'No, no, the king is dead, he killed him, he doesn't get the crown,' I hear. 'The king is dead, but he receives the crown nevertheless,' I argue. 'No, he doesn't. Yes, he does. No. Yes.' We take a look in the manual. I get my way. I feel like a half-wit spoiling the fun for everyone else. Like an accountant eager to ruin someone's holiday.

I feel very, very awkward. Eventually a third discrepancy with the rules comes up. 'You're going to kill me,' I say, then hide under the table...

***

Two weeks after the holiday is over. People are returning home from vacation, there are meetings and visits in my hometown of Gliwice. I receive Bogas and Dagmara, a married couple from Tarnowskie Gory. We're playing *Verflixxt*, and we're not even five minutes into the game, when another charming rules issue comes up. I want to move the bird and the pawn every time a question mark is rolled. Bogas wants every player to pass his or her token to the player on their left. Multidej shows off his German and quotes the manual. Dagmara cuts him off by saying that she graduated in German philology. Merry munches on some crisps, sits back and enjoys the whole scene.

Eventually, both Bogas and I shake our heads and give up on the whole fuss. It is settled – since we're playing in Gliwice, we'll play according to the Gliwice interpretation. We're having tremendous fun, unaware of the fact that both versions, Bogas' and mine, are wrong, which turns out to be the case a couple of days later. A few days after that a final, irrefutable translation of the game's rules makes its way into my *Verflixxt* box. And a week later, over two years after I had bought *Verflixxt*, I have the uncommon pleasure to play it according to its genuine rules. The match is sweet, a breath of fresh air, and is an entirely new experience. We're all satisfied with this new version of *Verflixxt*.

***

The number of games I have played not according to the rules is overwhelming. There was a period when virtually every board game I played, I played according to my own custom rules, since I would go and mix up and change things recklessly time and time again. Rules are eight, sixteen, and often twenty pages long, thick with text, full of sentences and every single one of them meaningful. Full of words, that are not just decoration, pretty feint or accurate metaphor. It's a dozen or so pages of simple and precise rules, full of indicative sentences describing how to play the game.

Miss only one and the game is out of control.

And a king's ransom for the one who has never overlooked a sentence, who has never missed an exception, who has never misinterpreted an example.

And so, to celebrate the beginning of the holidays, I have an offer for you. Take the rules of your favorite game and read it very, very carefully, one paragraph at a time. There's a chance that you will find a detail or a few proving irrefutably, that you've been playing it wrong all along.

Now make sure to play it according to the game's genuine rules. Experience the taste of freshness, discover new possibilities in your beloved board game, and name the new rules 'Trzewiczek's expansion'. It applies to any game. It is my gift to you.

Why do I enjoy boardgames so much?

WHY DO I LIKE TO MEET MY FRIENDS

AND SPEND WHOLE AFTERNOONS LEANING OVER BOARDS?

WHY DO I LIKE BOARD GAMES?

I've been wondering recently what makes me a fan of board games. Why do I enjoy them so much? Why do I like to meet with my friends and spend entire afternoons leaning over boards? I've written down some obvious answers.

I like to hold a new box in my hands. I like to unwrap it, eagerly look inside, and pick up the tiles sheet. I like to pick up the board, unfold it and examine it from all possible angles. I like to touch the pawns, the dice, and dip my fingers into all that colorful stuff. I like to hear the magical clicking of the tiles being pushed out of their cardboard sheet. I like to tear the wrapping seal off a deck of cards... Ok, I'm lying now. I don't like unwrapping cards.

I like the moment when a new game ends up on the table. Those frantic moments when players fight for pawns and argue who takes the green ones and who the yellow ones. When they trace the board with their fingers asking dozens of absurd questions. Are the yellow cubes built in these buildings? Can I play a bricklayer family, since I have the red pawns? I'm playing with the yellow ones, so being the Chinese I should get double the number of pawns, may I? And so on, and so forth. Madness. A new game means big expectations, a lot of positive emotions and joy in its purest form.

Oh, and cake is also a reason why I like board games. The cake and the tea biscuits. I like board games with a board so big, that there is no more space for the cake and the biscuits left on it. 'I'll hold it', I say and put the bowl of biscuits next to me. I sip my tea with my hand among the different sweets. Biscuits are usually brought by Multidej, pastry by Bogas and Dagmara, and chocolate in large quantities by Salou. Eventually it all ends up in reach of my hand. And I will plainly admit – these are some of my favorite moments.

I like to know about games. I gather this knowledge by various means. I browse through foreign web sites looking for information, pictures of new releases, fans' opinions and professional reviews. I read Swiat Gier Planszowych (The World of Board Games magazine) from cover to cover. I roam sites like Games Fanatic, BGG, and many more, absorbing information, ensuring that my need for knowledge is appeased. Unfortunately, it never is. And that's why I discuss games.

I debate with Tomek by mail, bragging about what I've played, telling him what is remarkable and what to avoid. I like long, sincere men talks, when we talk about our Better Halves and prove to ourselves that our attitude towards games, not theirs, is the appropriate one. It most certainly is. I like the 'Skype' chat with Pancho, when we indulge ourselves in all kinds of gossip, from recommendations, to comments regarding recent publishers' news. I debate every Monday, in the club, talking to Mst about games, asking for his opinion on various titles.

What I also like about board games is writing about them. Like here, now. When I sit at the computer in the evening and share my passion with you. I like the fact that, thanks to board games, I could start the board game club in Gliwice, that I could organize 'Pawn', a magical event. Smiling gamers come from all over Poland to attend 'Pawn'. I like the fact that I always misinterpret the rules and as a result I can always play one game according to two or three sets of alternative rules. I also like how the boxes form such marvelous piles...

Actually, what I also like about board games is the fact that you can play them too. But I get the feeling that that is one thing I could manage without. Without biscuits by the table, without email debates with Tomek, without piling up boxes on the shelf it would be a lot harder for me...

AN APPEAL TO WOMEN

Tomek reports what's up in Warsaw: 'We also played *Boomtown*, we played it till we dropped. The folks like it for its interaction. The women won. Same with *Manila* – there was always some woman with the most cash at the end, and boats with which men never arrived. Some kind of conspiracy.' A week earlier he wrote: 'Asia wins in *Adel Verpflichtet* every time. I have no idea how she does it.' Two weeks earlier it was my turn to flood his inbox with my sorrow, to report with sadness that I had been crushed by Merry in *The Pillars of the Earth*.

I have a regular correspondence with Tomek. We comfort each other and feel for each other, sharing our true astonishment for our Beloved Women and their unfair game table practices. Let's say it out loud – women do not play fair.

When Tomek sits down to play a game, he has a plan. He has a strategy planned out in order to arrive at a win, and he follows that idea. You can see it in his every gesture and every word. You can hear it in a triumphant 'Ha!' shouted after an especially successful move. You can see it in the proud way he reaches for his glass of wine or how he hits his fist against his knee after an especially successful move.

Asia lacks all these sincere gestures. She smiles innocently and we let our guard down. Asia asks for a glass of wine or some tea biscuits.

She won't admit to having a victorious plan, she won't betray it with a gesture or any other sign indicating that behind those glasses of wine, behind those tea biscuits there is a machine rising. A machine that is about to crush me, crush Tomek and every other man at the table. It'll flatten us like a steam roller. Women do not play fair.

As for me, my mouth doesn't shut as they say. I comment, give advice, tell off and mock. I live the game, I live every placed tile, every played card. I live more with every turn, to the point where every opponent knows what to do, what not to do. I live it so much, that towards the end of the game everyone knows what the person to my left is supposed to do. Even the people living across the street know it.

Women pretend that the game doesn't interest them that much. Merry manages to feed the kids, help both daughters with their homework and even do the washing. The board? Oh, she'll move two pawns, play a card and goes back to pretending that something else has her attention. The dog needs walking, the canary needs water. Sometimes the deception is of epic proportions. I say deception, because it's all a smokescreen. This nonchalance of moves, this apparent lack of involvement, it's all there just to cause us to let our guard down, to make us not take her seriously. To allow her to stay unnoticed, underestimated, secretly striving for victory.

She always does it, and week after week we let our guard down. There's admirable mastery in it, and insincerity deserving condemnation. Women do not play fair.

If things do not go well for Tomek, he literally breaks the board with his forehead. He leans over it so deep, as if he wanted to move the pawns with his stare, to make them reconsider and get out of the spots that were reserved for him. He raises his hands to the sky imploringly, and frowns back at the pawns. Tomek does not approve of those opponents' moves that cross him. And he demonstrates this lack of approval to everyone around. Including Mr. Kowalski, the neighbor from Nr. 3.

Asia doesn't wave her hands. She doesn't hit her knee. She doesn't eyeball other players, inviting them to share the drama that's happening on the board. Like all women she calmly accepts what consecutive turns bring, calmly adjusts her plans and step by step gets closer to victory. Of course we, the fair playing men, have no idea such plans

WOMEN KEEP WINNING!

exist at all. She doesn't fret and fume, doesn't waste strength on rubbing her forehead and doesn't brood over other players' sins. Asia, and all other women with her, plays calmly and is carried to victory by her serenity. Women do not play fair.

I'm not asking you to stop winning. I've got enough pride not to beg for mercy or a handicap, for letting some of my, or Tomek's plans succeed once in a while. No, we don't want your mercy. The only thing I'm asking you for, our Beloved Better Halves, is to at least pretend that you had to make an effort to defeat us. Don't make it look so easy. I'm asking you. Begging even.

I AM A LUNATIC

I rush into the house, toss my briefcase into the corner and run to my desk to get some sheets of paper. 'Daddy, daddy!' Lena's voice comes from the kitchen. My daughter runs through the hallway and hugs my leg. 'Merry, take her!' I shout in the direction of the kitchen and pass the kid to her mother. 'How about a good afternoon?!' I hear. 'I'm not here.' I answer and rush into the kids' room. 'Nina, give me the paint set, quick!' I command and run into the bathroom to get some water. 'Daddy, daddy!' comes from the kitchen. 'I'm not here!' I shout back. I pick up the paint, sheets of paper, a brush, water and get to the table. 'Ignac!' Merry is angry and now I'm going to get it. 'I'm not here, don't talk to me,' I answer, risking my life and start to cover the paper with paint. Have you seen Close Encounters of the Third Kind? Then you know what's going on. A nutter covering sheets of paper with drawings. Merry with the kid in her arms stands behind me, ready to hit me. 'Give me three minutes and I'll say good afternoon. Now I'm not here, please.' I say through my teeth and keep painting in blue, red and grey. One, two, three sheets of paper. They all fill up with notes, drawings, and arrows. 'I live with a lunatic,' Merry mutters to herself, and returns to the kitchen. My daughter cries. She wants her daddy. Nina brings more sheets of paper. It takes me three minutes to fill up six of them. I spilled everything I had in my head,

59

everything I came up with during a half hour drive. I didn't waste a single idea. I managed to put everything on paper. Phew. I get up, relieved. 'Darling, I'm back! How's your day?' I shout in the direction of the kitchen. With a squeal, my daughter runs to me. There are six sheets of paper wet with paint lying on the table. It's the groundwork for *51st State*, a card game that is going to debut in Essen 2010...

***

I sprained my ankle and had to go to the changing room in the middle of the match. It hurts like hell. It's way past eleven at night. I hope I won't finish my evening in the emergency room. I drink water and patiently wait for the game to finish. My mind goes to *Basilica*, a game which I've recently been testing and helping improve. A solution enters my head after a short while, one which I've been trying to find for days to no avail. I sit in the changing room, it's almost half past eleven at night and suddenly all the pieces start to fall into place. I have nothing to write it down on, I can't make notes, damn it. I pick up my mobile and write a text message to Merry. 'A choice of 3 helpers, a brigadier for two peasants...'. A few minutes pass. An answer comes: 'What?!' I might have woken her up. 'Write it down on a piece of paper on my desk, please.' A few moments of silence and another text message arrives. 'I live with a lunatic.' I don't deny it. The idea works and is going to be implemented in the final version of the game. From what I can tell, *Basilica* will be released in Essen this year.

Fortunately, the ankle wasn't that bad either. No trip to the emergency room necessary...

***

Sunday afternoon – a curse for many men who have to sit through a boring dinner at their in-laws. I have armed myself with *All Flesh Must Be Eaten*, a roleplaying game devoted entirely to zombies. I read a number of chapters, I look at the drawings, and the afternoon lazily drags on. Eventually I pick up a notebook and a fountain pen and start to scribble. No big deal. Zombies walking alongside railway tracks, people at some barricades. I write down a few rules, like that a zombie

Witchcraft, 2008. The only game I created (together with Michał Oracz) and I'm still willing to play anytime.

moves one field back when hit, that zombies in single file don't step back, or that different shots inflict different wounds... The afternoon drags on. I have five pages filled with rules and ideas for cards. A few days later I take a prototype to work. A few months later the game is released in Poland under the title '*Zombies*'. It becomes very popular, receives four additional prints, a release in Germany and a sequel – *Zombies2*. Lazy afternoons can be surprising...

***

I have an incredible job. I make games for a living. I buy shoes for my kids and realize that I have the money because people buy games that I've made. I pay my telephone bill and realize that I have the money because someone likes my ideas and has purchased *Zombies* or *Stronghold*. I have a pork chop with chips for dinner and I can afford it, because I made *Witchcraft*. I support my family thanks to ideas that come to my head. In the strangest places and times.

I am a lunatic. A bloody happy one.

THE POTENTIAL OF A PROTOTYPE

I have 30 cards. Each of them has a red watercolor mark at the top and a blue mark at the bottom. Each has a name written on it. One is called Guardhouse, another Petrol Station, and another Bunker. I take all thirty of them and go to the board game club in Gliwice.

Asiok is the first to arrive at the club.

'Come in, let me show you something,' I tell him and take out the cards.

'A new prototype?' he asks

'A brand new one,' I say and deal both of us five cards. 'It's set in the Neuroshima universe, a post-war world with a Mad Max feel to it. We're the leaders of some organization with the aim of expanding our power. Every turn we scan the horizon in search of interesting locations. There are three ways of making contact with a location. You can assault it to immediately get a lot of resources or you can start collaborating and start getting a smaller amount of resources every turn. You can also incorporate it into your micro-country by building a road. In this case you use that location to its full extent. OK?'

'OK.'

Asiok looks at his five cards.

'Ignacy, these cards are blank.' He shows me his cards marked with paint with names on them. Yeah, like I have never seen them before.

'Imagine that there's something on the card. Show me what you've got. Here, you have a Petrol Station. If you assault it, you'll get lots of fuel at once. Or collaborate with them and get one fuel every turn. Or build a road here and you can start selling that fuel to me.'

'OK, I'm assaulting the station and take lots of fuel.'

'And I have a Watchtower. I'm going to make a road.'

'What does a Watchtower do?' Asiok asks me.

'I have no idea, to be honest. Let's say it defends you from attacks.'

'Can you attack one another?'

'For the time being you can't. Keep playing. What's in your hand?'

'I'm playing the Barracks; it'll give me soldiers. I too will make a road and it's now part of my country.'

'OK, I'm contacting a Pub, it'll give me one hit man every turn.'

Five minutes later we run out of cards. I'm collaborating with the Pub and the Refinery. Asiok has a Barracks, and has also assaulted the Petrol Station and the Arena. We have no idea what these cards do. It's irrelevant at this stage. It's the potential that counts.

'And?' I ask, 'Can you imagine what it's going to look like in the future? Would you enjoy such a game and its features?'

'If you do a good job, there'll be lots of choices. Players will have plenty of potential moves.'

'Did you have any vivid ideas? Did you feel you were assaulting locations and signing contracts, and that it has nice atmosphere and makes sense?'

'Yes, there's potential here. Bring a new version next week.'

***

I show the game to a few other people that afternoon. I play with Sheva, Mst, Allchemik and Korzen. The last two, to my amazement, after playing a weird, made up match against me, asked me for the 30 cards and played a game against each other, also making up the rules to the cards as they went along.

It was clear to see – *51st State* had something interesting about it. When someone asks me what this game is about, I won't have to say: 'Well, it's a new kind of pick up and delivery with a twist...'

I won't have to tell them: '*51st State* is the four hundred and fifteenth take on territory control mechanics, where the players fight for field advantage...' I won't be embarrassed by saying: '*51st State* is a game using deck building mechanics known from *Dominion*, but but then slightly different...' It's not a boring, three hundredth variation on a popular theme.

I made a game about which I can say something interesting in two sentences. *51st State* is a game in which players look for locations and are able to make contact with each and every one of them in three different ways. You see an Old Radio Station and you can invade it and steal their equipment, you can start collaborating with them and use it every turn, or you can annex it and it becomes exclusively yours.

Two sentences sell the mood of the game. Two sentences to show the mechanics and hint at a multitude of choices and tactics. Two sentences showing that it's a great piece of tangible storytelling fun.

That day I started to believe in the potential of *51st State*. I saw that this vivid idea works, that people played a card game with cards which had no rules on them. And yet they could imagine what was happening and enjoyed it. I enjoyed it too. It was something new. Not another euro game with cubes, not another *Dominion* clone. Something different. Assault a location, collaborate with it or annex it, making it part of your territory.

One card – three colorful, strong storytelling outcomes.

INITIALLY THE PROTOTYPE DOESN'T WORK.

HEART ON THE PITCH

Initially the prototype doesn't work. It's ugly, boring and crashes often. It takes a lot of effort to find people willing to play and test it. Friends try to avoid it, preferring other games from their collections. Then, after a few months it starts to work. It doesn't crash anymore. You are happy with it. After many weeks your game finally works. You start to think about sending the prototype to a publisher.

Stop. Before you do that, you need to answer a question.

Before you send a prototype to a publisher, answer this question – Is my game the best game in the world? If the answer is 'No', you can throw your prototype away. I'm being serious. If you, yourself don't consider the game to be excellent, outstanding, the best in the world, then what are you counting on? Do you think others will? You don't love it yourself, so what do you expect others to think of the game?

Every time I sat down to work on *Stronghold*, tinkering with the rules, drawing boards, sketching the outlines of a castle, at every point, every afternoon, there was one thought on my mind: 'Here comes *Stronghold*, the best board game in the world.' I would create new actions for the Invader, or design new actions for the Defender and mutter: '*Agricola*, you are about to lose your crown, *Stronghold* is coming.' Everything I did for the game, I did believing that I was creating the best board game in the world. I would lie awake at night tossing and turning, trying to come up with ever better design choices, so it could beat *Puerto Rico* and all the other top games.

I'm a realist. I know that *Stronghold* won't ever reach the No. 1 spot in the BGG charts. I knew it even when I was creating it. But being realistic has nothing to do with it. When you design a game, you clench your teeth and do everything you can to create the best game on earth. There is no other way. Your game will revolutionize the market, it'll win you both the Spiel des Jahres and the Deutscher Spiele Preis, and your name will become synonymous with genious. That's all that matters to you.

It's a bit like in a basketball match. When you face the Chicago Bulls with Michael Jordan on the court, you realistically estimate they'll win 96-72 or 101-78. But down in the changing room you believe in victory. You've trained to the limit, your team has been fine-tuned, your coach is good, and so you believe you can win. You have to believe you can defeat anybody. The game starts, you lose two quarters and before half time it becomes obvious that you've failed. But it doesn't matter. Training, belief, heart on the pitch, hope and strength matter.

The game was released and didn't reach No.1 on BGG, and that was to be expected. But back then, when I was pulling all-nighters, creating it, preparing it for publication – I believed it would be the best board game in the world. I believed it to be excellent, that people would love it, and that it was unlike any other released game. Original, interesting, thrilling.

If you've finished working on your prototype and plan to send it to a publisher without yourself being able to describe it as original, interesting, thrilling and if you don't believe yourself that it's the best game in the world and it's going to enter BGG's top 10, then you should take that game and bin it.

There are thousands of average games in the world. Publishers expect the best of the best, and won't settle for less.

HEART ON THE PITCH 2

In the beginning the prototype doesn't work. It's ugly, boring and crashes often. It takes a lot of effort to find people willing to play and test it. Friends try to avoid it, preferring other games from their collections. Finally, after a few months, it starts to work. It doesn't crash. You are happy with it. After many weeks it's finally there – your game works. You start to think about sending the prototype to a publisher.

Stop. Before you do that, you need to answer two questions. The first one was covered previously, today I will discuss the second one.

When your friends visit you, do they ask you if they could play your prototype? Do your buddies say: 'Could we play your prototype today?' If they ask for it, everything is just fine – send it to a publisher. If you have to persuade them to play it – throw it away. It's not worth releasing.

A few weeks ago I came back from my holiday in Croatia, which I spent with friends and a large group of children. The friends are board game fans, so we had a good number of board games in the trunk of the car, besides swimming trunks, fins and goggles. The friends brought *Dominion* and *Small World*, and I brought *Neuroshima Hex*, *Galaxy Trucker*, *Doom*, *Tichu*, *Havana* and the *51st State* prototype.

Throughout the entire trip we played one game of *Small World*, one of *Havana*, five games of *Tichu* and over 20 games of *51st State*.

I didn't suggest playing *51st State* once, I always waited for others' suggestions. I wanted to see how quickly they would get bored with it, what its replayability was, and how many games it would take for them to get fed up with it and want to play something else. Honestly, I didn't suggest playing it even once. And the game made it to the table over 20 times...

On the last evening of the holiday Piotr came to our room. They'd packed their stuff, put their children to bed. We'd packed our belongings as well, and our children too were in bed. We were planning to leave for Poland at 7 AM the next morning. It was 10 PM, the last evening of the holiday in Croatia.

'How about a last round of *51st State?*', Piotr asked.

'With please' I said.

51st State is a winner and I'm feeling good about it. We had brought sensational titles with us, the board game elite, ranging from *Dominion*, to *Small World*, to *Havana*, to *Galaxy Trucker*. And yet in Croatia they all gathered dust. The game on the table was *51st State*, time and time again.

My answer to the question: 'When your friends visit you, do they ask you if they could play your prototype? – is 'Yes'. Yes, I sent *Small World* back to the shelf. Yes, my *51st State* made *Dominion* stay in a suitcase all holiday. Yes, due to my card game we only played *Havana* once during the entire holiday.

Yes, *51st State* is ready to be released. The prototype has been tested, pitted against the giants, which it has trapped on a shelf. If your prototype is not up to such a trial, don't send it to a publisher. Nobody is going to release a game worse than the ones already present on the market. You have to be better. You have to lock the giants in their cupboards. You have to make the competition retire early.

FUN WITH TESTERS

Browarion, Grzech and I finally had the chance to meet and discuss *51st State*, three weeks after they had taken one of the prototypes home with them. They live in Wroclaw, while I live in Gliwice. With 200km between us the only contact comes courtesy of Skype. But thanks to Pionek, a convention for gamers, we can finally meet and play together.

'The Merchants are too powerful,' starts Browarion. 'They win all the time.'

'It's possible. You got the deck for testing, didn't you? I never noticed it and perhaps you have found a way to win the game by using the Merchants.' We sit down and play. 'Take the Merchants,' I say.

Browarion took his Merchants. We played the three player version. The Merchants came third.

'Let's play again,' said Browarion. Again we sat down and played. The Merchants came last. We played again. The Merchants came last for the third time in a row. I'm tempted to tease him but Grzech beats me to it.

'I told you, but you wouldn't listen. Don't look at the nations, look at the players. When we played in Wroclaw you didn't lose to the Merchants, you lost to me. I told you that.'

***

The match has been on for a good fifteen minutes now. Piotr has been moaning like a slaughtered calf for a good fourteen minutes.

'The Merchants are too weak. They can't do anything. The contracts are not useful to me, three spots and that's it. This needs to be changed.'

'Stop moaning and play.'

'But they are. Can't you see that?!'

'How many points do you have?'

'14.'

'How many do I have?'

'14.'

'So will you, please, stop moaning?'

'I'm being serious. Do you know how I struggled to get these 14 points?'

Another 10 minutes passed like an eternity, since Piotr managed to fill every single one of them with more moaning.

'The Merchants are weak, what a joke! The contracts' spots are blocked and you're all over me.'

'Stop moaning, just focus on the game. I'm going to finish in the next round.'

'I would finish too, but with those stupid Merchants I stand no chance. Maybe a fourth contract spot, or a universal resource instead of this stupid fuel would give me a chance to compete.'

We were done ten minutes later.

'How many points do you have?' I asked.

'36. And you?' he asked.

'36.' I answered.

'See? I barely managed a draw!', he is moaning again!

'You have more cards left in your hand, which means that you have won. That's the tiebreaker. The Merchants have won.'

'Do you realize how tough that was? The Merchants are too weak, I'm telling you!'

***

After another series of tests I discard the Baby Swift from the deck. The players have too few cards in their hands to afford discarding two more for a victory point. Baby Swift is an unplayable, dead card. We play without it and everything works well until the next rule change. Now the players have more cards in their hands, so Baby Swift gets another chance. It comes back. We play subsequent matches and indeed, Baby Swift makes more sense now, even though it seems to be one of the weaker leaders. Players tend to put their money on Borgo or Greedy Pete, while Baby Swift is usually a second or even third choice. I make notes and analyze everything, constantly monitoring which cards come into play and which ones are regularly ignored during the draft. It seems to me that Baby Swift walks a thin line between being popular and being unused. It's a little too weak to be a hit and slightly too strong to simply be discarded from the deck. It gets used sometimes.

In the meantime Michał Oracz prepares another version of the prototype for me – new graphics from the illustrators have come in. We can finally play with the original Baby Swift artwork that will appear in the final game. The graphics are insane. Another wave of matches and tests commences.

Baby Swift is the most popular leader in the game now. It's on the table every single game. It's always the players' first choice.

I haven't changed a single rule. I only changed the graphics.

***

Testing games is crazy fun. You get dozens of contradictory conclusions and pieces of information. Every tester tries to pull in their own direction. Each one has a different view. Each one expects from the game something different. One tester plays well, another one is not that good. One tester claims that a certain faction is powerful, another finds it the weakest. Testers from Wroclaw catch me on Skype in the evenings and ask me not to listen to testers from Opole, because *51st State* doesn't need negative interaction. Opole rings me and says that the players from Wroclaw are little girls, and *Neuroshima* is for big boys. Wroclaw writes that Opole is biased, since they prefer war games there. And that the Merchants are too weak.

Game reports. Result files. Statistics. Opinions and claims. A continuous flow of information.

I sit and filter through it. I pick recurring remarks. I check and thoroughly analyze opinions which seem to appear on a regular basis.

And everything else... into the bin.

I HATE *STRONGHOLD*

Around the end of July 2009, shortly after all bloody tests were finished, I realized that I had grown to hate *Stronghold*. I was fed up with it. I hated it. A few weeks later, when the production of the game started – a ride with no handlebars, I hated it even more. My heart would stop at the mere sound of the word 'stronghold'. I was fed up with phone calls from Rebel (the biggest board game distributor in Poland) or from the office regarding publication. Of course, back then I didn't really know that much about hating *Stronghold*. Essen was the place where I finally learned what hatred really means.

Essen 2009 was tough. I have a gift for composing words into nice sentences and expressing emotions, but I fail at adequately describing the horror of this fair. An unbelievable job held in the rhythm of a 15 minute monologue game presentation. The game is about a siege. One player plays the role of the Defender, the other is the Invader... Trzewik, this customer would like an autograph, would you sign it? Yeah, I'll sign it, defenders know that there is no chance to save the castle.... Trzewik, this man is from a Portuguese portal, and he'd like an interview. OK, let him come back in an hour, they fight only for two reasons... They earn time for women and children to escape from the castle... Trzewik, this guy asks if you have a publisher in Brazil. I don't know, ask Rebel, I've no idea what they've signed so far. And they fight for honor, for history. They want to be remembered as brave warriors. Spartans, you know... Trzewik, this guy asks if the box contains a manual in French. No, it doesn't, the French edition is made by IELLO, the defender has altogether 30 cubes representing soldiers. The invader has 300. The question is not if he will break into the castle, but when... Trzewik, a guy from Phalanx Games just came in asking for some detailed rules. Trzewik, that woman from the Czech Republic is back, what do I tell her? Have Multidej explain the rules to her. And have her leave a business card, I'll call her back later today. This is the Glory board. It represents the glory that players have earned. It's cool, I'm from Poland, you can explain in Polish. I can't do it in Polish, I've been doing it in English for three days now. At the beginning of the game the Invader has 10 glory points... Trzewik, Petr is asking if you can lend them a copy for the night in the hotel. Yes, I will. After every turn of the game, he will lose one... Trzewik, Rebel says the Dutch are interested in 2000 copies, wicked! Cool, the chronicle will say: 'Well, the defenders fought bravely'... Trzewik, do you want to swap our games?

We would get up at seven, eat breakfast, drive to the fair, explain the rules to *Stronghold* for 10 hours straight, return for the night, hit the bed dead on our feet and repeat it all again the next morning. Yes, I really hated *Stronghold* then. There was no way in the world anyone could talk me into a game of *Stronghold*.

'Trzewik, you have to do an expansion, you know that, right?', Piotr Katnik, Rebel's boss asked me at the fair. 'It's an absolute hit – the game of the fair, we will sell everything we brought with us. The stock we have in Poland will sell before the end of the year. People will want an expansion. You've made a hit, now you have to make an expansion.'

I knew that. I knew that bloody well. And I hated *Stronghold* even more. The thought of setting up the board and testing an expansion made me sick.

'I need a break of a few months, then I'll make an expansion. I promise.' I answered.

I kept my word. I made an expansion for *Stronghold*. I put all my heart and talent into it. I bent over backwards to satisfy the play-ers, to give them a new story, a new chunk of emotions and joy. I'm looking at this expansion, I'm looking at the testers and I know I did a splendid job.

And now I know that before it was just teasing. Oh yes, now I do truly hate *Stronghold*.

IS IT AN EXPANSION OR IS IT A NEW GAME?

It's Cedric's fault. We met in a hotel in Essen, in 2008 – two people from Portal and three people from IELLO, and discussed our publishing plans. I told them about a game I wanted to design – I told them about *Stronghold*. It was October 2008, the very beginning of my work on that game. I spoke about the huge numbers of troops, about hordes of skeletons and orcs storming the castle.

At the end the skeletons didn't make it into the game, but the orcs did. The game was shown in Essen and I had a lot of fun with it.

I met Cedric again in October 2009. We discussed publishing plans again. I told him about the *Stronghold* expansion. I told him I was considering replacing the orc cubes in the Invader's army with the undead.

'That's it!' he exclaimed. 'The last time you spoke about *Stronghold* I imagined hordes of skeletons. It's going to be great. I wish you had included skeletons back then!'

I returned home and started working on the expansion. I wanted to make the expansion similar to those modules of *Race for the Galaxy*. You buy a box with four, five sets of new rules inside, pick the one you like and ignore the rest.

I started with making 8 new Heroes fighting in the stronghold. That was easy since *Stronghold's* realm, the realm of Monastyr, is very rich. It didn't take me long to think of distinctive features for Heroes from the realms of Kord, Gord or Doria. Interesting rules would immediately pop into my mind. Some weeks later the first part of the expansion was ready for testing – a new set of game transforming Heroes.

Next in line were the Invader's cubes. I looked at the white, green and red cubes thinking what I could do. The white ones became Phantoms, the red ones became Vampires and the green ones... The green ones were Skeletons. Rotten Skeletons, sort of, but Skeletons nevertheless. What do Phantoms do? They... fly. Bang! A rule just got created – white Invader's cubes don't need free spots at the walls since they don't need ladders to fight. Vampires? They spread vampiric power and strengthen the Phantoms. Skeletons? You kill one and its bones return to the game. It's not discarded but reused (back then I didn't know in what way yet).

There you go, nice and easy.

I looked at all the Invader's actions very closely to check whether they fit the undead army. Some of them were inconsistent with the plot. I mean, do Vampires use Saboteurs? Do Skeletons use Saps?

At some point I should have given up on analyzing whether Skeletons made Poisons, built ladders or Trebuchets.

I didn't. I delved into it.

Does a Necromancer send his troops to build machines? No. He casts spells and uses powerful magic to summon nightmarish ballistae and catapults. He doesn't need wood or nails, he doesn't send ghosts to paint banners. He summons it all with his magic. Very interesting possibilities started to appear. I was entering the fascinating world of spells. There were Warhammer Battle books with Vampire armies on my table and galleries of undead artwork opened on the computer screen. Wherever I looked, there were cemeteries and skeletons.

I couldn't stop myself. The board started to fill up with cemeteries, strigas, mists, ghost illusions... The situation was getting out of hand, especially when I looked into the castle one day. How about new ways of defending against the undead? I created Priests, Exorcisms, stakes for the vampires and tower crossbows...

After a few weeks it turned out that the whole idea, modules of different new rules in this expansion might as well be scrapped. The undead would grow and expand with every working day, slowly taking over the whole expansion. There was no more room for anything else. I would create new actions for the Invader, new actions in the Castle and slowly realize that this idea was big enough to simply dominate the expansion.

Today the testers don't say that *Undead* is a good expansion. Today they say they're playing *Stronghold 2*. An entirely new game. And that it's great. Much better than the first one.

VISIT

I spent approximately 35 minutes at Bazik's house, as we were in a hurry – Merry, me and Folko. We managed to have some tea and play two short, very quick games. That visit cost me €10, because Merry absolutely fell in love with the first of the two games. So it resulted in an order and a money transfer.

I spent 90 minutes in total at a two-day convention in Belk. You could say that I just dropped by, said hello to friends, had some tea and went back home. Costs? 40 zloty for petrol and as much again for *To Court the King*. To be honest I didn't even play it. I just came in, saw the cards, listened to how it was played and went home. Then I switched on my PC, turned on the browser and ordered the game from Rebel.

Seriously, one is scared to go out, to meet with friends. Wherever I go, costs follow me. One visit and the shopping list gets longer, a game catches my eye and the money drains from my wallet.

Anyway, what can I say, I'm no innocent myself. I take a heavy toll too, you could say. You come and visit me, or invite me to your place and you can be sure it'll cost you dearly.

I came back from Warsaw yesterday, one evening at friends', and those friends are now €10 down. They rather liked *Adel Verpflichtet*, which I had brought with me to show them. One meeting with Folko at 'Pawn' where I demonstrated *Verflixxt* to him and his wallet suffered. I invited Bogas and the visit cost him a bit too, you know – petrol, delicious cake, and of course the decision to buy *Mall of Horror...*

Unfortunately it's like good games yell out at us: 'You must have me, you got to have me!' And with friends it's like they never put some unplayable Pinocchio on the table, oh no! You have barely crossed the threshold, barely managed to agree to a cup of tea, when you hear they have recently bought a fantastic game which you just have to see and play. And so the best game from their collection ends up being played, the pearl they want to show off, the wonder making you think on your way home: 'Great, awesome, I have to get this game too.'

I'm looking at my shelf and see these titles – *Dungeon Twister?* Bazik's fault. *The Pillars of the Earth?* Pancho's doing. *Heckmeck?* Revenge for *Adel Verpflichtet.* Yes, it's the friends from Warsaw...

How are you supposed to socialize? How to meet gamers? How to visit friends? Seriously, it's scary. With terrifying consequences...

THROUGH THE AGES

It is called *Das Verrückte Labyrinth*. Known also as *The aMAZEing Labyrinth* or just *Labyrinth*. Published by Ravensburger in 1986, the game was then republished in 16 different editions and gave birth to a whole range of games with *Labyrinth* in their name. A true classic. A best-seller. And – what is more – the board game of my childhood. I do really have no idea how it got into my home. It was deep communism in Poland then, no board games in the stores. It must have been sent to us in some package from Germany. I don't know. It doesn't matter. What matters is that I spent countless hours with it.

It's been more than 20 years now. I still remember playing it with my parents and brother. I still have a photo in my old photo album of me playing the game. I loved that game. I believed then I would play it until my dying day. Unfortunately, I grew up.

I was introduced to Role Playing Games, I got to know hundreds of exciting things to do. My box with *Labyrinth* disappeared. Lost in time. The adventure had finished. It seemed forever. Well... Not forever.

Three years ago my friend Adam brought his copy of *Labyrinth* to our gaming club. When I saw the box, I felt a thrill. My eyes opened wide. My heart beat stronger. Memories returned to me of days long past. I asked Adam if I could borrow the game. 'No problem. Have a good time with your kids,' he said and I took *Labyrinth* with me. It was nearly 15 years since I played it last.

It was amazing. It was like time travel. I was sitting at my table, with my kids and I was playing *Labyrinth*. Magical moments. Could I – 20 years ago – have believed that when I would be an adult, I would still play this game? I couldn't.

We played for a few months. I sat with my kids and together we fought to find the best track to our goal items. Every single game of *Labyrinth* with my kids was like the best game ever. I had a great time.

Unfortunately, finally my kids grew up...

I've just packed my *Labyrinth* away in a box. The adventure is finished, again. My son wants to play *Galaxy Trucker*, Nina wants to play *Kingsburg*, and in fact, *Descent* is their favorite. 'Dad, *Labyrinth* is a kids game,' they say. It is over. *Labyrinth* goes to the bottom of the wardrobe. I will miss it for a few years.

My youngest daughter is 2 years old. In three years I will pull out the box from the wardrobe. I will put it on my table. And again, I will be the happiest man on the planet.

I AM GETTING BETTER

It was last summer, two months before the release of *Stronghold: Undead*. I was running a demo of the game during the Polish convention 'Kaszubkon'. It was Ryslaw, a big fan of *Stronghold*, who was playing *Undead* with his opponent – Tele – that night. At some point Ryslaw said: 'Damn, this is great. *Undead* is much better than base *Stronghold*. I loved *Stronghold* and this one I love even more.'

'It has to be better. I am learning. I gain experience. Every year my skills improve,' I said. I really believed that *Undead* was better than the base game and I really believed it had turned out exactly how it was meant to. Every new project has to be better. My *Zombiaki2* is better than *Zombiaki1*, *Undead* is better than *Stronghold*, *The New Era* is better than *51st State*. That's how it works.

I really do like all my games. Almost 10 years after the first release of *Zombiaki*, I still like the game and I am proud of it. I love *Witchcraft*, I am damn happy that I designed *Stronghold*. But I also know that if I would do them today I could make them better. Every month I play new games. I observe other players playing my games. I read game blogs, reviews, I am in the very center of the gaming world. I learn. Every day I am getting better as a designer.

Today I am writing about this because this week I did something exceptional (from my point of view, anyway).

Last year I designed *Pret-a-Porter* – an economic strategy game about the fashion world. It was published in Poland in late November. (A few days ago it was nominated for Game of the Year in Poland.) In *Pret-a-Porter* there are more than 50 cards (representing employees, buildings, contracts) with text on them explaining how they work. Since November I was worrying about an international release of the game. It was impossible to make an international edition of the game with so much text on the cards!

For many many months we were – here in Portal – unable to change *Pret-a-Porter* into a language-independent game like our previous releases. It was a huge problem for a small company like Portal. For months we were trying to create some iconography for the game and we failed. We failed over and over again.

In fact, a few weeks ago we finally decided to do an only English edition with English text on the cards. We saw no other option.

Last week I decided to sit down once again with *Pret-a-Porter* and try one final time.

Last week I sat down and this time it turned out I could do it! I designed icons for *Pret-a-Porter*. I finally did it. I finally got rid of the text. I am happy as hell. I have been waiting for this moment since last year.

I am happy to know that I am improving. Every single week.

I'M DONE

This is it. I am done with *The New Era*. From now on, for the next few months I will be – literally – bombarded with only bad news. I had a great time designing the game. Creating new cards. Finding new strategies. Watching testers having fun or not having fun. Recording results and spending hours analyzing. That was fun. That is my beloved job. That is why I wake up every morning with a smile on my face.

This is it. From now on no more smile on my face. From now on I wake up and think, what is the bad news today. What's coming?

The Cover
The cover of the game is in progress. I am eager to see it. And you know, I have no idea if I will like it or not. I like the cover of *Stronghold*, but I don't like the cover of *51st State*. I like the cover of *Pret-a-Porter*, but I don't like that of *Witchcraft*. It is like Russian roulette. So I am waiting. Will I like the cover to my own game? Not for certain. It may be good news or bad news for me.

The Components
You wouldn't believe how many things can happen with components. Components are bad news generators. That is why I will not be able to sleep well until Essen, when I will finally have my game in my hands.

When *Stronghold* was being printed I was terrified – there were so many tokens, I was absolutely sure that something would go wrong. No chance that everything would go smoothly. Luckily, there were no mistakes with *Stronghold*. But we got screwed a year later, with *51st State*. You can easily forget about one tiny token that is used in very rare situations. Your graphic designer may misunderstand some token and design it with some errors. Your printer may screw up the cutting of the tokens and they will be poorly cut. Every time I open a box with a new game of mine I am terrified. What went wrong this time...

The Rulebook
OK, the rulebook for my game... Need I write anything more? This is hardcore. I can't write rulebooks. I hate rulebooks. I cannot sleep because of my rulebooks. You can't understand my rulebooks. OK, let's stop it. No more about rulebooks.

Demo Games
I love to teach how to play my games. During conventions I spent endless hours showing my games to new players. I also love the Essen fair. This is the moment, this is a culmination of many months of hard work. I love this crowd, I love meeting players from all over the world, I love this great event.

And still, at some point it will turn into a nightmare. I will be happy doing a hundred demo games. I will be happy doing another hundred demo games. But at some point I will no longer be able to talk about the game. No more. And I will be forced to say: 'I hate my game. I really do.'

Joy will finally return. Two years after publishing *Stronghold*, I am thinking about playing it again. I think I like the game again. I no longer hate it.

In three years from now I will like *The New Era* again. I only have to wait.

I CREATED A MONSTER

A long time ago in a faraway galaxy my wife didn't play board games. Then I showed her *Cash & Guns* and *Citadels* and she began to play games. My mates were jealous. My wife played board games. Lucky me. It was a great time. But months passed...

One day I came back home and said that I had just sold *Adel Verpflichtet*. 'What do you mean, you sold it?! Why didn't you ask me?! I like that game! Bring it back!' She was serious. Man, I felt like I had been hit by a sledge hammer. She was damn serious. I wasn't allowed to sell *Adel Verpflichtet*!

That day I discovered that there are games she likes. Games she wants us to have at home. That was something new. That discovery cost me €14. I had to buy *Adel Verpflichtet* back again. No longer was it my games collection. It was our games collection from that moment onwards.

We were in a car, driving back from a board game convention in Vienna and talking about the games we had played there. 'I want you to buy me *Ingenious*,' she told me. She was serious. She was damn serious. She wasn't talkin' about flowers. She wasn't talkin' about perfume. Nor about a new dress, a handbag, or a ring. She was talkin' about a board game. She wanted me to buy her a board game. Wow!

That day I discovered that My Wife – like my true gamer friends – fell in love with new titles. She played a new game, loved it, and consequently wanted it. That was something new. That discovery cost me €20. I had to buy *Ingenious*.

Early September, a few days after the holidays. The kids were asleep, silence at home. My Wife asked me to play *Race for the Galaxy* with her. In previous weeks we had played more than 50 games of RftG. I was sick of it. I could not even look at the game anymore. 'No thanks,' I said. I heard my voice and I couldn't believe it. I had just refused to play a board game. My Wife wanted to play a board game. I didn't want to play a board game. This was crazy.

That day I discovered that I am not the only one at home who asks to play board games. And what is more, perhaps, I am not the truest gamer at home. It seemed that My Wife was more 'geeky' than me. I was scared. Terrified to be honest.

A few days ago. 'Do you want to play *The New Era*?' she asks me. No way. I am sick of it. She knows it. I had been refusing to play it for a few weeks already. I was asked to play every day and I refused every day. This was a determined defense. I refused and refused. This was terror. No seriously, I was pushed into a corner, terrified. I felt like a 'geek's wife', forced to play a board game every single evening.

'Never mind,' she says 'I asked Tycjan to come over. He will play with me'. She is serious. She is damn serious. They play *The New Era*. I only watch. I don't play. I can't believe this is real. I can't believe this is happening.

This is my latest discovery. I have created a monster. There is a truly dangerous geek living in my home. Please help me!

ME AND MY

BOARDGAME

MONSTER!

THE RACE BEGINS

Last year there were 650 games released in Essen. A year before – as far as I can recall – there were 630. This year, the record probably will be beaten again. How many of these 600 games will make it onto players' wish lists? How many of those games will manage to attract attention and leave players without €20 or €30? How many games will be remembered after a year or two?

Essen 2010? *7 Wonders, Vinhos, Troyes, Inca Empire, London.*
Essen 2009? *Dungeon Lords, Stronghold, Egizia, Small World.*
Essen 2008? *Dominion, Ghost Stories, Le Havre, Space Alert.*

600 new games each year. But only a few of them stay with us for a really long time. That's the truth. The brutal and cruel truth...

Authors and publishers of these upcoming games are at their stands today and they start preparing for the most important race of the year. The race for players' wallets. How will they try to seduce these players?

The Theme
Great, a new theme? If you have a good theme, you will attract players, even if they've never heard about you or your publisher. Tell them that you are doing a 4X game, and you will immediately gather a true circle of science fiction geeks. And believe me, this is a very good start.

In 2009, I published my game *Stronghold*. It had a great theme. That was it. The game blasted off like a rocket.

A year earlier, in 2008, I presented in Essen a game called *Witch-craft* – wizards fighting each other. Have you ever heard about this game? Well...

A Reputable Name

Have you made a name for yourself and now people will buy every single game of yours? An author with a recognized name is a treasure. People look for his new games, they are driving a spiral of excitement and expectation. Gossip, shots of a prototype, sneak peeks from test games...

If your name is Martin Wallace, Uwe Rosenberg or Bruno Faidutti, you are probably a lot less scared before Essen than a less experienced designer like Ignacy Trzewiczek.

A Publisher's Reputation

Does your publisher have a known brand? Did previous games establish his reputation? Does he have a bunch of regular customers who return year after year for his titles? Such a faithful player base is a blessing.

In 2007 Portal was an anonymous company from an even more anonymous country, Poland. I remember the words from a *Neuroshima Hex* review written by Greg J. Schloesser for Counter magazine: 'I honestly do not know much – OK, anything – about the gaming scene in Poland but if *Neuroshima Hex* is any indication I am impressed.' At that time, in 2007, we started from scratch.

Today, five years later, the situation is much better. We are those people who made *Neuroshima Hex*, *51st State* and *Stronghold*. I feel that, through our hard work, step by step we are getting closer to the famous brands in the board game industry, slowly approaching publishers like CGE, Fragor and Ystari Games.

Demo Games and Prototypes

Has your game been presented at large cons? Did you take your prototype and test it at every possible convention? If so, that is good. There are session reports on various sites written by people who were lucky and played the game before its release. At opiniatedgamers.com there are the first opinions, BGG is full of rumors – someone out there has been playing your game, and someone is sure to have seen that it is damn good...

Your game becomes a legend. You are a lucky bastard. There is nothing better than a rumor saying that there is a great game out there, and there are some players who have played it and apparently the game is great...

Traditional Marketing

If you can afford it, you will have banners on the most important board game websites. You'll show off the cover, display your preorder offer, bundle offer or whatever. Finally, you get some attention, and you are well positioned in the players' minds. You show up on their wish lists. Your cover is instantly recognized, the theme is well known, even – in the end – people will remember your stand's number and the Essen promotion price of your game.

Not very subtle, but it does its work.

The Visual Aspect

Okay. Moment of truth. Raise your hand if you have purchased a game solely based on an amazing cover, not even knowing a single thing about its rules. It was just the cover. The board? It's the same thing. Raise your hands if you have never heard of Mr. Menzel. People buy stuff with their eyes. Clothes, furniture, games, food, it doesn't matter.

Zack & Pack? I knew nothing about this game, yet I bought it. *Golden Compass*? I saw the board and bought the game. With a good illustration on the box, a player has zero chance to prepare a proper defense. He sees the artwork and he buys the game.

Two years ago we paid a hell of a lot for *Stronghold's* cover. For *Pret-a-Porter* we hired Tomasz 'Morano' Jedruszek. It was the most expensive artwork in the history of my company. This is the guy who works for FFG on a daily basis and who made covers for *Middle-earth Quest*, *Battles of Westeros* and *A Game of Thrones LCG*. This is the guy.

A good cover is like Aikido. It throws a man to the ground and simply makes him defenseless.

Preorders and Promo Stuff

A great preorder offer? Some promos for free? This is something that can make all the difference. If a customer has the choice of two games and cannot decide which one to pick, it is better to have some kind of limited bonus in your game, an Essen special. A few extra cards. Some additional tokens. A unique extra miniature figure.

The player will rather take the game with the special Essen freebie. The second game he will probably buy after Essen. Or not at all.

Luck

Or maybe you just have a remarkable stroke of luck? Perhaps your stand in Essen – by accident – will be positioned next to some famous publisher and you will have a great deal of traffic? Or maybe you'll manage to convince people that you printed only 500 copies of the game and that they have to buy it now or never? Or maybe the game will be played by the boss of a big US game store in a hotel lobby in the evening? Maybe he will fall in love with the game? And the next day he will buy 250 boxes from you?

Conclusion

You'll need it all. In Essen, six hundred new games will make their debut. The famous BGG Geeklist 'Top Ranked Essen Games' contains slightly more than 20 titles. So – 20 games make it and the other 580 go overboard and you will never hear about them again. This is brutal. This is cruel. This is Essen.

In 2009 and 2010 I had the honor to have my games in this list of 20 games.

However, this year – after doing *Neuroshima Hex*, *Stronghold* and *51st State* – I'm going to Essen with a game about clothes and fashion. *Pret-a-Porter*. Fashion. Clothes. Hot models.

This is crazy. I can't believe it.

And you cannot imagine how scared I am.

In 2011 and 2012 Pret-a-Porter has been nominated to Polish Game of the Year Award, Origins Award (best boardgame) and International Gamers Award (general strategy).

PRET-A-PORTER IS LIKE
AN OLIVER STONE MOVIE...

Martin – a player from the board game club in Gliwice - won all of his games of *Pret-a-Porter*. He battered his opponents left and right, without exception. I was always there. I watched. I took notes. Sometimes I changed something in the rules for the sake of balance. I watched in silence as week after week Martin was leaving all the other players empty-handed. Asiok, Ryu, Sheva, Tollis, Arti... Anyone – and I really mean anyone – who sat down to play with him, got up after two or three hours with his or her head bowed. Again and again, Martin had more money than all the other players put together. Cornering them. Strangling them. Bringing them to the brink of bankruptcy. He profited from the opponents' blood and tears.

In the end I couldn't stand it anymore. I put my notes aside. I also put aside the role of the game's author who's carefully watching the ongoing test plays. I'll play, I said, and sat down to play with Martin.

I won the first fashion show. I dominated him, got the biggest number of Stars, the largest amount of money and bright perspectives. I had carefully watched Martin's moves throughout all those previous plays. I knew how to beat him. I knew *Pret-a-Porter* like the back of my hand. My game. My territory.

Things went in an absolutely unexpected direction during the next round. Martin blocked me in the Warehouse, where materials can be bought. He did not need those materials. He did not have to do this. But he wanted to.

My clothing company took a huge tumble. I obtained materials from a different source, but this slip had cost me a lot, and the second fashion show turned out to be far less successful than the first. I would have managed to get on an even keel with Martin, and stand to fight as an equal during the third show if I had been battling an opponent who might allow that. I was not. Martin blocked the Credit House and once again left me standing at the door of the Warehouse. It was as if he was holding his knee to my throat, and pushed harder each time he put his pawn on the board.

I finished the game with a disastrous score. Martin battered me so hard that I didn't know where to look.

We played a rematch a week later. This time I managed to hold out a bit longer. The killing blow did not strike me until the last quarter...

***

In 1987 Oliver Stone made an amazing movie with Michael Douglas called 'Wall Street'. It deals with what money can do with people. Wall Street does not show the well-behaved businessman. It cannot be associated with peaceful economic games in which we buy raw materials, change them into goods and sell them at a profit. Wall Street shows the struggle, the betrayal, shows that money is – just like firearms – a tool that can kill.

Pret-a-Porter is like Oliver Stone's movie. It is dynamic, aggressive and players feel the ever increasing pressure of their battle for victory in each subsequent round of the game. It has been achieved in a simple manner – there are four moments of scoring (fashion shows) during the game and you have to be ready for each of them. You must be active all the time. You need to have a short-term strategy (for the upcoming show) and a long-term one (for which show to press the most and on which ones to allow your company to catch its breath). You have to watch your opponents' moves and try to thwart their plans – win the show for which they prepared the most, get at least a tie in other scorings – don't allow them to win and get a large amount of cash.

This is a real fight. Here, you count your money and calculate what you can afford. Do you have the funds to pay the maintenance costs of the company? Do you have enough to purchase materials? Or enough funds for your business development? And if you have the money, you calculate even more. What if? What if I employ a model thus increasing the maintenance costs – will that thwart my enemy's plans? What if I opt for more expensive materials – will I outdo my opponents in the show where quality counts? Can I afford to buy more materials in advance in order to dominate the following show? Will taking the credit for those actions pay off? Will I manage to invest money and win the next show?

You are facing a constant barrage of choices. You observe your opponents. You find weaknesses in their businesses and snatch the employees they need up from under their noses. You inflate your maintenance costs to draw your opponents into a trap, into an exhausting race for dominance in Public Relations. You check your expenses constantly and analyze what else you can afford, how far you can risk taking the struggle for the collection's other features. It sometimes comes down to bluffing and sometimes it is a merciless stab in the back. You train your employees, develop your buildings, take a loan, pick materials from three quality classes, set up short--term contracts and construct permanently built buildings.

When I sat down to work on this game and I wrote down the feelings and emotions that I wanted to evoke from the players, I did not expect that I could achieve all of that. That my skin would tingle before each move. That I would hold my breath before my opponent's actions. That I would swear like a sailor or a tavern wench when I saw what my opponent was doing and how much damage he was causing me with his actions.

I have to admit, *Pret-a-Porter* turned out to be much better than I expected.

HOW I DIDN'T WIN SPIEL DES JAHRES

It was all in the blink of an eye. In a single moment my new game was ready. It just came to my mind and it was brilliant. I was so excited. Players are shepherds and have to have the biggest flocks of sheep. Different tiles have sheep with different colors, some tiles have wolves who eat sheep. Your aim is to gather groups of 4 sheep in one color. Simple, easy, great.

No orcs. No mutants or tanks.

No 'Trzewiczek-style' game.

Spiel des Jahres jury, here I come!

I took brushes, I took paints and started to make a prototype. I have a huge range of Citadel paints, very expensive, but very good. I wanted my prototype to look great. I used Citadels paints, and I painted 32 tiles with green paint (sweet meadows!). I drew 158 little sheep and then I painted all of them (yellow, white, blue, and red). It was great, I was imagining myself coming to the office, showing the prototype to the guys and telling them that I'd just designed a great game! It took me the whole night. Nearly 5 hours of painting little sheep.

The most beautiful prototype I have ever seen.

It was way past midnight, but I was so proud of myself. It had to be a hit! I was excited. I didn't go to sleep. I took a box of chocolate, and painted it grey, and then I drew a meadow and some sheep on the front cover. It was awesome. Spiel des Jahres jury, watch out 'cause here I come!

Finally I went to sleep.

I woke up the next day. I was so proud. I ate breakfast and sat at the table to play my game. The first test. I was very excited. This was the first time in my designer life that I was about to play a test game of such a beautiful prototype. So I played.

Well, not exactly. I didn't play because it didn't work. It didn't work at all! I was sitting at the table and couldn't believe that I had spent the whole night painting sheep, without first checking if the rules made any sense.

That's how I didn't win Spiel des Jahres this year. And today's advice from me to you is – first test, then paint, my friends. First test, then paint...

You'll find my beautiful sheeps on the colour pages in the book.

CAN I BITE YOUR GAME?

The first time I came across the term 'cannibalize' in a board game context was in 2007 during my interview with Bruno Faidutti for the Polish magazine 'Świat Gier Planszowych' (The World of Board Games magazine). I asked him how many games he had in his collection. 'More than five thousand, but it's hard to say. I cannibalize many games.'

'What?' – I asked, clearly not understanding what he meant.

'I cannibalize. I take components from other games and use them in my own prototypes. Thus, a lot of my game boxes are incomplete and will never be playable again.'

'Oh,' I said. That was something absolutely new to me. And it was only two years after my conversation with Bruno, when – during my work on *Stronghold* – I finally fully understood what he meant.

***

I have used game pieces from two copies of *Mykerinos*, two copies of *Glik* and one copy of *Elasund* for my *Stronghold* prototype. I added a cartload of Lego bricks as walls, pots, cannons, hooks... The castle looked like a vast construction site. For a moment it even seemed possible that five incomplete game sets and a pile of my son's bricks

were going to be enough for me to work. Unfortunately... During the final stages of my work on the game I had to send the prototype to testers, and had I not discovered a store with wooden beads I would have been in serious trouble and Ystari would have been over the moon with twenty more copies of *Mykerinos* sold to me.

While working on *Prêt-a-Porter* I cannibalized copies of *Arkham Horror*. This game has wonderful cash tokens. I borrowed one of the copies from the club in Gliwice, the other one was lent to me by Tycjan from Opole. I tarnished the sanctity of this game during my works on *Stronghold: Undead* – I used *Chess* pawns for priests. I also made use of the green cubes from *Space Alert*. They worked so well that eventually we contacted our friends from CGE and with their help the final version of *Undead* is equipped with the same type of cubes as in *Space Alert*, though their color is not green but blood-red...

My game *51st State* was created using game pieces from *Light Speed*, and *Light Speed* was created using IKEA glass markers. I designed *Witchcraft* with the use of damage indicators from the first edition of *Neuroshima Hex*, and *Machina* (Machine)... To be honest, I created *Machina* from scratch, all by myself. It was my first game. I didn't know then that one should steal the components, and not cut them out with scissors from cardboard...

✳✳✳

I write about this as now I'm working on *Robinson Crusoe*. Without even noticing it, I have cannibalized my favorite CGE game – the wonderful and crazy *Galaxy Trucker*. And now, not only can I not fly into space and experience great adventures there – I also had to splash some paint on my brave Czech astronauts for the sake of *Robinson*. In my prototype I needed meeples in four different colors, so I had to paint the astronauts. Their resemblance to Neil Armstrong is lost.

Galaxy Trucker is one of my son's favorite games. What will I tell him now? How can I admit to what I have done? Even if I finish my work on *Robinson* pretty soon, even if none of the astronauts are lost during the tests and they all eventually return to *Galaxy Trucker's* box, space trips will never be the same again. *Robinson* has left a considerable mark on them...

IGNACY TRZEWICZEK

THERE IS NO SUCH CARD!

The Essen fair has ended, the stress level has dropped - finally a moment to catch my breath. I can play the newest releases, see what other authors have prepared, breathe in any new ideas. I'll note any interesting solutions that may be inspiring and I'll allow my mind to be stirred by others. Sometimes – quite unexpectedly – something completely new is born from all this commotion.

Finally, after several plays, I had a moment of inspiration. Oh yes. And as a result, within two weeks after Essen a brand new prototype made it to our table. We played. Turns came and went. Step by step Merry was gaining the upper hand and finally I could see nothing was going to change anymore. Two moves before the end of the game it became clear I was beaten. The prototype seemed to be cool, yet the cards had little to do with balance.

I drew my last card. It was called Commandos, yet there was no text, symbols or rules of any kind on it, only a title and cool graphics. I didn't have the slightest idea what the mechanics should be, only a cool title, so I just tossed this card into the deck. Very clever. 'Trzewiczek style' they call it – the story always comes first, and later you'll have time to worry about the rules.

And so I drew this stupid Commandos card and with a poker face I put it in New York, saying 'Commandos. I won.'

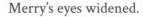

Merry's eyes widened.

If I would have had to buy her some contact lenses right at that moment, they would have had to have been the size of the bottom of a jar.

'What?' she asked almost completely speechless.

I had lost miserably. The only thing left for me was to tease her a little bit. 'Well, I drew Commandos. Didn't I tell you that when Outpost draw that card, they win? And so I won.'

Merry didn't believe what she had just heard. 'There is no such card.'

I kept a straight face. 'There is. As you can clearly see here. Commandos wins the game.'

'Ignacy, there is no such card!' Merry furiously rushed to the other side of the table, grabbed the Commandos and threw it away. The card landed on the window sill. 'Ignacy, there is no such card.'

All I could do was burst out laughing.

Two days later, the Commandos has its abilities described. Maybe it does not win the game, but... but still this is my favorite card in the whole deck.

MONEYBALL

Somewhere in the beginning of January, *Steel Police* got on my nerves and I snapped. The army had caused an unbelievable carnage on the table in the Portal office. Won most of its battles. You see, it was not only winning all the battles – it was beating other armies into a pulp. Again and again. The results' sheets from the months of December and January are filled with such results as 17:0, 12:0, 13:1, and even 7: -4.

The day when we were to finish our tests and start preparing files for printing was getting closer and closer, and the way the army was behaving was just plain ridiculous. Finally, I couldn't stand it anymore. I called Michał Oracz.

'Michał, come to the Portal office. We must weaken the *Steel Police*. What we have here is a mockery of a balance.' – You see, as of January 2011 Michał no longer worked at Portal, and we had to ask him to visit our office if we wanted to sit down together to discuss *Neuroshima Hex*. And it seemed there was a lot of discussing to be done. Michał had to come. Two hours later he stood in the doorway of our office.

'Michał, the army is not balanced. I have the entire file of results – and it looks very bad.' I greeted him, quickly getting to the point.

Michał took the printout. Looked. And nodded.

'You're playing it wrong.'

I gaped at him.

'What?'

'The army is balanced. You're playing it wrong. Who's making sure the rules are upheld during the tests?'

'Maciek.'

Michał sat down with Maciek and began to question him about the rules. It was just like an exam. He came up with the most bizarre situations and asked how he would interpret them. Such things had never been seen before at Portal. The situation was peculiar.

Maciek passed the test. He answered all the questions. And so Michał invited him to play.

'Show me how you play the *Steel Police*.'

Michał took the Hegemony, and comfortable secured victory over the *Steel Police*. They played again. The *Steel Police* lost a second time. They played a third time. The *Steel Police* was beaten a third time in a row.

'The army is balanced. Learn how to play,' he said simply and went home.

***

A few days later *Steel Police* tests moved to the next stage – we sent the file to the most trusted and experienced *Neuroshima Hex* players in Poland. Those guys who win tournaments. The ones that go to conventions and organize game shows. The biggest *Neuroshima Hex* geeks in the country. They were obliged to send daily reports of their results, along with a description of their plays. The results ended up in Michał Oracz's mailbox and a copy was sent to me. I followed them closely. They made my hair stand on end.

The *Steel Police* was nigh unbeatable. The results were frightening. We had 3 weeks to the tests' closing date and the army had absolutely nothing to do with balance. It won all of the battles.

During this time I called Michał almost every day.

'Michał, did you get the latest results? We are weakening the army, huh? Introduce a few changes, please.'

'They have to learn how to play against this army. It is balanced. Do not change anything.'

Just 3 weeks were left. I was close to a heart attack.

***

Have you seen Moneyball? There is an extraordinary scene where Brad Pitt, the manager of the Oakland Athletics, is called into the office of the chairman of the club, together with his assistant, to answer for the current situation. The team results are a catastrophe, Oakland has lost eighteen games in a row. They are last in the group. The chairman asks what they're going to do.

'We estimate that we will begin to win in mid-season.'

'I beg your pardon?'

'The team will start to win in mid-July. We will qualify for the playoffs. Trust us, please.'

They've just lost the eighteenth game in a row. Trust us. Yeah, they certainly have nerve.

***

It was several days ago. Two weeks before the final deadline. After the weekend I received another large batch of *Steel Police* results from our testers. Resigned, I gave it a glance. And immediately, I mean immediately grabbed the phone.

'Did you see the results?!' I almost shouted into the receiver.

'They've learned how to play,' Michał replied calmly.

The bastard was right. He had known from the start what would happen.

'They've learned how to play,' I said and nodded. 'They've learned how to play...'

In this story Michał played the part of Brad Pitt. I was only the chairman who withstood the pressure and didn't start to tamper with the team ...

THE JOKES ARE OVER

It's January. Joke time is over. It is time to begin Operation: Essen 2012. It's been like that at Portal for years now. October is fair season, and in particular Essen of course, in November we take a break and rest, and in December we look through our ideas, prototypes and the different sketches we've collected over the past few months. Then comes January.

In January we begin working on prototypes and new ideas. We analyze and discuss them. Finally, we choose the one we think is the best and has the biggest chance for success. The one we want to present during the next Essen fair.

In 2007, before Essen, Michał Oracz showed us his newest game prototype. He worked on it for the rest of the year and in January 2008 it was all clear – we would publish a game about a duel of wizards. This is how *Witchcraft* was born.

In 2008 I had my idea for a game about a castle siege. It is a couple of years ago now, but I still remember how nervous I was when in January I came to the office with a big sheet of paper with a castle drawn on it to present my prototype to the rest of the guys. We decided the game had great potential. We began working on *Stronghold*.

We closed 2010 without an idea for a new game... We closed it with a finished game. That year we published *Pret-a-Porter* in Poland.

We didn't plan to publish it in other countries, but as weeks went by, that idea became more and more tempting. The reviews in Poland were incredible. Everyone was asking us the same question: 'Are you going to Essen with this?'

We didn't want to do that. *Pret-a-Porter* was completely different from our previous games – its theme was so strange. And the cards – they were full of text. We also knew that if we would sacrifice another few months to prepare an international edition of the game, we wouldn't have anything new for the Polish market.

It was a tough nut to crack. You have a great game on the table and a hard decision to make. Do you start working on its new edition? Or maybe put it on the shelf and begin a new project?

Finally, we decided to give *Pret-a-Porter* a chance at an international career. We had a lot of time. We designed the best, most legible icons in the history of Portal. We balanced the game even further. We added some new, great cards. We went to Essen 2011 with a fantastic game. Thanks to many months of hard work we polished *Pret-a-Porter* in the smallest details.

What's more, we still had a lot of time to rest, clear our heads, look for new ideas and prepare for the next year.

It's January 2012. Again, there are a lot of prototypes on our table. We have a second expansion for *51st State*, we have a two-player card game, we have a new cooperative game, and a couple of new armies for *Neuroshima Hex*. January is the month of playing and discussing. A month of decision making.

In a few weeks our publishing plan will be ready and approved. We'll begin Operation: Essen 2012.

IT'S A MYSTERY

Have you ever seen Shakespeare in Love? As the bubonic plague breaks out, the Crown orders the complete closure of all theaters in London. Suspended performances, unemployed actors, the audience in despair. And what about an investor who has put all his money in the show? He is furious to say the least. Catching the play's director on one of the streets of London he demands an explanation. Now! He has invested a lot of money and was counting on fat profits. And what now? A disaster! Theaters are closed! The guy is hungry for blood.

What are we going to do now?! – he shouts into the director's face.

Nothing, sir. – the director calmly responds. – It always works out in the end.

How?

I do not know, sir. It's a mystery.

***

From the sole beginning I had a problem with interaction in *51st State*. Testers said the game was fun, gave a nice feeling of satisfaction from playing it, but – what a shame – no interaction. Again and again I heard the same thing repeated to me: cool and interesting, but you know, lacks interaction...

117

As I subsequently added draft rules, open production rules and the Thieves Caravan, the complaining voices slowly died down. Testers saw that I was changing the game, trying to add at least a bit of co-operation between players.

What's more, I wrote articles explaining why there is no room for burning, raping and pillaging in *51st State*. In my posts on BGG I argued that if players were allowed to kill each other it would destroy the game, everything would fall apart and turn into one big scrap.

People read my posts, agreed with me, admitted that perhaps I was right...

But you know, the fact remained that there was little interaction...

***

Peter caught me in Essen. He is the guy responsible for the distribution of all Portal games, you know. I make games and he does the business part. I'm trying to invent the best game I can and he's doing everything to sell 50,000 copies of the game. Or more.

So he caught me and told me, as if speaking to a child – Trzewik, *51st State* is a hit! Publishers are fighting for the rights to an English edition. And they are asking whether there will be any expansions. Will you make an expansion?

I will.

Great, great. It's a very good game, everyone likes it, you did a really good job.

Glad to hear that.

Only you know what? – he pauses to choose his words carefully – I do not want to impose, but is there a chance that in this expansion...

...there will be more interaction? – I finish for him.

Exactly. So you've heard there is somewhat too little interaction?

Yeah, so I've heard.

Damn interaction.

It kept me awake at night for more than half a year. – There will be an expansion. There will be interaction. Don't worry.

***

We returned from Essen. It was the end of October. I had absolutely no idea what to do with the interaction. No clue. No conception was born in November either. And still nothing at the end of December.

I caught my friend and like-minded spirit from France on Skype.

Hi Yann, what's up on the French forums? Are people playing *51st State*? Any opinions, or suggestions for the expansion?

Yes, they play and discuss a lot. They do like the game, but they are all complaining about the lack of interaction.

Yann, gimme a break, will you?

***

Having no idea how to implement rules that would add interaction in October did not worry me in the slightest. In November I still remained calm. I believed – like Geoffrey Rush in Shakespeare in Love – that everything would be fine.

Yet, in December, two months after Essen, I still had no idea how to handle the interaction. I think that Peter, my distributor, slowly began to worry at that time.

I rushed into January in an unwavering good mood, although, with the end of the month coming closer even I began to worry.

Maybe believing that everything always somehow works out is a bit illusory? Maybe Geoffrey Rush's words are a load of crap? Gosh, I love that movie, but maybe I shouldn't base Portal's publishing plan on a movie?

Do you have the interaction element ready? Designed many cards, huh? – Peter inquired.

None. – I replied. February was coming soon. – I still have no idea. But I'll manage.

How?

I do not know, Peter. It's a mystery.

***

I play football every Monday. We play in the hall late at night until we drop. I get back home just before midnight and I sit in the darkness for a good two hours, gasping for breath and letting the adrenaline slowly flow out of my body. Hot tea, a dark house and silence. I can analyze all my plays then, getting angry with myself about all the opportunities that I've wasted and replaying in my mind all that worked out nicely.

Thoughts wander in and out of my mind, my body barely alive... One moment, I don't even know when, I have the rules for interaction. They're just there. Suddenly. I don't have the slightest idea where they came from or how they got inside my head. I walk cautiously through the dark room, trying not to trip on one of the toys scattered on the floor. I get to my desk. Paper, pen, three sentences, two drawings. Done. I carry out the tests in the morning. It works. As easy as that.

How?

I do not know, sir. It's a mystery.

DESIGNING A GAME IS NOT A 9-TO-5 JOB

I don't know how other designers work. I don't know if I am a freak among designers or if I am a classic example. But I want to tell you what it looks like. How it looked with *Robinson*. I spent my last year on the Island. Seriously...

***

For me 2012 was the year of *Robinson Crusoe* because for the last 12 months I have only read adventure books. I really mean it. I read a lot of Jules Verne novels. I read all novels I could find about castaways. I read all books about survival I could find. I also read comic books and I – certainly – watched all movies I could find that were about deserted islands or castaways.

I read about dozens of ways of making fire. I read about building shelter from almost nothing. I read about how to find water, I read how to find North without a compass, I read everything I could. I am – without a doubt – one of the most educated persons on this planet... in terms of castaways...

If, by any chance, you are on a deserted island, just call me. I will teach you how to survive. You don't need to worry.

***

For me 2012 was the year of *Robinson Crusoe* because every single weekend of this year I had the prototype of the game set up in our living room. Our home was literally paralyzed by *Robinson*. The game is big, it covered nearly the whole table in our living room (and I have to say – we have a big table). Because of *Robinson* we had mess on that table for every single weekend of 2012. I played it all the time, every single weekend, and I drove my wife crazy with the tokens, cards, notes, dice and all other gaming material that was living with us that year.

It was like a part of our furniture. We had a sofa, we had a table, we had chairs and we had *Robinson*. It became a part of our everyday life.

***

2012 was the year of *Robinson Crusoe* for my whole family. The kids have grown – it was an entire year! – and day in day out they saw and heard about *Robinson*. They discovered the story. They played the prototype with me. They played live *Robinson* all the time. They built a real shelter in our garden (OK, I helped them a little), they spent countless hours in our garden hunting imaginary beasts, strengthening the roof or looking for treasures. Without a doubt, if in 20 years I ask my kids about the summer of 2012, they will tell me, 'It was the time of *Robinson*'.

***

2012 was the year of *Robinson Crusoe* because it really touched our daily lives. We spent our holidays this year by the sea, and of course I had *Robinson* with me. The game was with us all the time. Sometimes it touched our lives in a funny way. I remember one Sunday a few weeks ago. I was a little late for dinner, I entered the room, and the kids were already eating and there was no plate for me on the table. I asked: 'Hey, what about me? I don't eat?!'

And I heard 10-year-old Nina's answer: 'You know, it is like in *Robinson*. There is never enough food... Today you get 2 wounds!'

Wow. That was accurate...

***

Next week I am in Essen. My adventure with *Robinson* ends. I will finally have left the Island. I will finally be free. I spent a year of my life there. It was great, but I think it's enough. It is time for you to visit the Island. I strongly recommend it. This is a great adventure.

ESSEN, BEHIND THE SCENES

Day 0 – Wednesday, 8:00 AM. Hulk.
Have you ever considered how all these games get to a publisher's booth? I'll tell you how - we bring them there. I may not look like Hulk, but this is exactly how it works – a transport company delivers a number of pallets of games to the conference halls and then we need to unpack all these pallets and somehow get all those games to our stand.

1500 copies of *Robinson*. 1000 copies of *Convoy*. 1000 copies of *Winter*. 1000 copies of *Dancer*. 1000 copies of older stuff like *Pret-a-Porter*, *The New Era*, *51st State* and *Steel Police*. Nearly 20 pallets all together.

And there are three of us to do that. The rest of the team arrives in Essen in the evening.

I may not look like Hulk, but to be honest, after day 0 and unpacking a few thousand copies of games I am not sure why the hell I don't look like Hulk. On Wednesday we carried a few tons of games. I talked with Petr from CGE – they had nearly 10 tons of games. They don't resemble Hulk either.

Well, some publishers look a little tired on the first day of the show. Try to guess why...

Day 0 – Wednesday, 2:00 PM. Wilson.
At 2 PM I have the demo of *Robinson* on BGG live stream. I go to the BGG stand. I am a little bit nervous. Have you heard about stage fright?

Yes, I have heard about it too. So I am there, but the BGG schedule has fallen to pieces. They have a 30 minute delay. I have to wait and trust me, waiting doesn't help. Waiting is making me nervous. Waiting is making me think about a few things... That English is not my native language. That BGG is running late and that I have to shorten my presentation because they want to decrease this time problem. That in a few minutes I am going live. Worldwide.

Sophie from Z-Man Games appears at the BGG stand. She greets me. She wishes me a good presentation. She will keep her fingers crossed for me. I tell her that I am prepared. I tell her that the demo of *Robinson* will be great. I tell her not to worry.

There is only one thing I don't tell her. I don't tell her about stage fright. Yes, it just got its grip on me and is holding me tight.

Finally BGG is ready. They give me a microphone. We can start. We start. I am no longer nervous. No care anymore about stage fright. I just do what I can do best. I talk about my beloved *Robinson*. And this is live. And worldwide. Yes, it is.

30 minutes later we are done. My mobile starts to beep every few seconds. Many friends from Poland send me immediate feedback. They say it was a good demo. I am happy. A few days later, when Essen is done I can finally watch it. *Robinson's* demo happens to be – as far as I can see – the most popular video from Essen 2012. 1800 views. Wow.

Day 0 – Wednesday, 5:00 PM. Z-Man's crew.
That day at 5 PM the demo guys from Z-Man came to our stand. We taught them how to demo *Robinson* and *Convoy*. Doing a demo during a convention or fair is not a piece of cake. There is no room for improvisation. This is something you have to prepare for.

We've spent the entire week at the Portal office training how to best explain the rules of *Robinson*. In the beginning it took us 30 minutes. Later that week we were able to explain the rules of *Robinson* in 10 minutes.

You need to remove everything that isn't necessary. Remove any rules that are not important at the very beginning. Remove all unnecessary details. Be focused. Be clear. Be understandable.

You have to remember one more thing – in Essen you will meet gamers from Germany, from France, from Italy, from the whole damn world, gamers for whom English is not their native language. Your demo has to be simple. Your demo cannot involve sophisticated vocabulary. Your demo has to be easy to understand for anyone who can barely speak English.

We spent an hour with the guys from Z-Man. We taught them a special set-up of the game, made for Essen, with the easiest events and cards. And we were lucky. The Z-Man crew consisted of a bunch of great gamers. They picked up things in a second. I was sure the game was in good hands.

Later on I visited Z-Man's stand to check if everything was going well and if they needed any help. They showed me that they had changed the set-up of the game a bit. They started the demo from the second turn so the game would speed up from the very beginning. It was a great idea. They knew what they were doing. There was no need to worry. I was happy.

Day 0 – Wednesday, 7:00 PM. Everything is set.

At 7 PM we were ready to go, 11 hours after leaving the hotel, 11 hours of work without a lunch break, a dinner break, or any break, for that matter. A few thousand games were ready for purchase at our stand. The demo of *Robinson* was live on the BGG site. Z-Man's crew was ready to present *Robinson* and *Convoy*.

We were tired. We were hungry. And yes, we were damn happy. Man, it's Essen. We had been waiting for this day for a whole year!

2008

PORTAL GAMES
AT ESSEN SPIEL

2014

ESSEN, BEHIND THE SCENES, PART 2

Day 1 – Thursday, 11:00 AM. Frank.
I have a demo game of *Robinson* scheduled with Frank Kulkmann. For those of you who may not know it – Frank is one of the most famous and respected German reviewers. He runs an amazing website at boardgame.de and year after year he reviews dozens of games that are released in Essen. His Essen reports are extremely popular in Germany. During these four days of the Essen Trade Show he plays scores of games and reviews them right during the fair.

How is this possible?

Frank reads rulebooks before the fair. He doesn't waste time by letting publishers explain the game to him. He just sits and plays. He's prepared. He's professional.

So, Frank comes to our stand. He sits down to *Robinson* with two other gamers who were also interested in trying *Robinson* out and... starts to explain the rules to them. Just like that, he sits down and he teaches them how to play. I try to help, but Frank says that he can handle it. I can go to the second table to present *Robinson*.

Yes, Frank is a pro.

Day 1 – Thursday, 01:00 PM. Tables, tables!
We have two tables to play *Robinson*, so 8 people can play the game
at a time. Is it enough? OK, try to guess. We are under a storm of
gamers. I made a huge buzz and now I am in trouble – we are being
overrun by gamers who want to test *Robinson*.

We need to react. We need to redesign our stand. We move tables
around, we take one table from Rebel, we put it all in a new order.
Now we have two tables to play and one table to explain the game
– a short explanation just to give an idea of how the game is played.
From the moment we make it available, till the very end of the Essen
fair it is crowded with people. We talk about *Robinson* all the time.

Three people are assigned to the explanation table. It's very exhausting work as you have to talk all the time, you have to talk loudly
because of the noise all around, and you have to repeat the same
monologue time and time again. We take turns every 30 minutes.
It's tough.

Day 1 – Thursday, 06:32 PM. BGG BUZZ.
I receive a text message from a friend from Poland. You are in 7th place
in the BGG Buzz ranking. Wow. We were so busy that I completely
forgot about this. I forgot that BGG was doing this poll to check
which game was the most popular. Our hall and our booth are far
away from the BGG booth. I am so happy that despite of this, some
players went there and voted for us.

I am very tired after 9 hours of explaining *Robinson*. However, this
news about the BGG Buzz gives me a new adrenaline boost. I am
thrilled that people like *Robinson*.

Day 1 – Thursday, 09:00 PM. Hotel tournament.
Before Essen my wife Merry scheduled a little tournament with some
gamers from Hungary: Gabor and Krisztina. Gabor had stated that
he managed to get 128 points playing *Winter* (he is one of our testers
and had *Winter* many months before its release in Essen). My Merry
couldn't believe it. She said she would meet him in Essen and kick
his ass.

Yeah.

Merry convinced our friend from Gdańsk, Hubert, to join the game. Two players from Poland, two players from Hungary. They were waiting for this moment for weeks, arguing on Facebook chat about who will win.

So they meet in the hotel. They sit at the table, ready to show who is the best *51st State* player in Europe. Ready to rock. I smile. I ask them: 'By the way, does anyone have *51st State* with him?'

They look at each other. I start to laugh. No one has the game. Brilliant.

Day 2 – Friday, 09:00 AM. Geeks play fair.

It's the second day of the fair. We no longer have problems with English, our demo games and presentations are smooth and fluent. The number of players who want to test *Robinson* is ridiculous. We decide that we are going to have to shorten the demo games. We ask players to finish after the 4th round of the game. They understand. They see the queue of other players who want to test the game. We were afraid how players would react when we asked them to stop after the 4th round, but these gamers are awesome. They understand the situation. They test the game, and then they make space for other gamers. Geeks play fair. Respect for all of you!

Day 2 – Friday, 01:00 PM. Interviews.

During Essen many people want to do an interview with me, want me to talk about *Robinson*. They don't know it is risky business to talk with me about *Robinson*. For Friday I have scheduled an interview with Paco from G*M*S Magazine. Paco asks me about *Robinson*, so yes, I talk about *Robinson*. And you know, when I talk about *Robinson*, this is like 'Fatality' in the Mortal Kombat series. You can't defend. You can't resist. You are unprotected.

Paco didn't know this. This lesson cost him €45. We finish the interview and then he buys *Robinson*. 24 hours earlier the same mistake was made by John Knoerzer of the BGG crew. He sat with me while I was presenting *Robinson* on BGG live. He shouldn't have let me talk about *Robinson*... Yeah, €45 from his pocket to mine...

Never ever let me talk about my games.

ESSEN, BEHIND THE SCENES, PART 3 (FINAL)

Day 2 – Friday, 03:00 PM. Going green.

At some point in the day our booth is visited by His Green Majesty Friedemann Friese. He buys *Robinson*. I congratulate Friedemann, joking that Friday has finally found his master and we have a good laugh. Then I have this crazy idea - let's take a photo together! Robinson and Friday!

Friedemann has a sense of humor. He immediately agrees. My Merry takes a photo of us. A few days after Essen I upload it onto BGG. Within no time we are on the #1 place in the BGG gallery. We have a nice souvenir from Essen.

Day 2 – Friday, 06:00 PM. Android Jan.

In my previous post I mentioned that on Thursday we decided that we did not only need tables for playing the game. We also needed at least one to present *Robinson* in just a few words. This was the hardest spot, it was the most exhausting part of the job, it was the place where the work was so tough that we had to take shifts. I mentioned this in a previous post.

Czech Games Editions had a beautiful big demo version of *Tzolk'in*. Always crowded. Always busy. From 9:00 AM till 7:00 PM. No break. No single pause.

This demo version of *Tzolk'in* was managed by one person. One. Just one.

I am not sure if he was a human. I'd rather say he was some kind of android. A terminator. A cyborg.

In the beginning we were working hard and he was working hard. But then we died (all 3 of us) of exhaustion. He didn't. A Czech android.

Somewhere around 4:00 PM it was getting ridiculous. It was his 7th hour of talking about *Tzolk'in*. Without a damn break.

At about 5:00 PM Merry went over to him and gave him a chocolate. We were afraid that he would – sooner or later – just faint. He said, 'Thanks,' but he couldn't eat it. He had to explain *Tzolk'in*. Without a break.

It was about 6:00 PM when we spotted that the *Tzolk'in* demo version was empty and the Czech android was gone! OK, he died, we thought. He was damn good. He worked for 9 hours straight without a break. Let him rest in peace... A few seconds later we realized that he was sitting with a group of players at the table and he was teaching them how to play *Tzolk'in*... This was crazy.

After the fair on Sunday, we walked over to the guy and congratulated him on his work during Essen 2012. His name is Jan Kudela. He is the hardest working demo guy I have ever seen in my life. And man, trust me, I have seen a fair few. Jan, if you are reading this, once again I'd like to say: 'You did an awesome job this Essen!'

Day 2 – Friday, 09:00 PM. Winter has come.
The second evening in the hotel. Hungarians against Poles. *51st State* competition. Krisztina and Gabor against Merry and Hubert. I am going to watch and be the judge, making sure there are no problems with the rules.

They look at me. They want me to play. They don't need a judge. They want to play with me.

I am tired. I don't like to play my own games. But what the hell, Essen is once a year. I play.

Krisztina plays well. Gabor plays very well. I am playing with the Merchants and I will have difficulty burning him down and stopping him. The other players are either blind or stupid not to try to get him and kill him. In the third round I finally feel I need to attack and my peaceful Merchants visit Gabor and start burning. It is at least one turn too late. He is already damn strong.

I am pissed off. I won't let some Hungarian player kick my ass! No way!

60 minutes later it turns out that I will. Gabor is fuckin' good. He kicks my ass. And Merry's, Krisztina's and Hubert's asses too. At the end of the game Gabor has more points than Merry and Hubert together. This is a knock out. I am second, but far away from Gabor.

Merry invites Gabor and Krisztina to Poland. They will visit us. Ass kicking is on its way. I don't think I can defeat that guy...

Day 3 – Saturday, 06:00 PM. Marvin Gaye.

I am starting to sound like Marvin Gaye. For 3 days we have been taking all medications we can to protect our throat and voice but now, after 3 days of presenting *Robinson* at our stand, they don't work anymore. Because of the noise in the halls in Essen you have to shout when you present or explain a game.

You can't shout for 3 days in a row without consequences.

So here they come. The consequences. I sound like Marvin Gaye. I kinda like it. Merry likes it too...

Day 4 – Sunday, 08:00 AM. It will be a hard day.

Half of our team has to go back to Poland. They were our supporters, but they don't work for Portal, they have their normal jobs and they have to go to work on Monday morning.

There are only 3 of us left at the stand. We are – however – not scared. For many years Sunday has been a boring day for us. On Sunday the halls are always crowded with average German families, not geeks. Games like *Neuroshima Hex*, *Pret-a-Porter* or *The New Era* never attracted them. On Sunday we were always bored and had nothing to do.

Soon it turns out that *Robinson* is interesting for German families. We have as much work as every other day. We are crowded. They want to play. They want to hear all about the game. The theme is very interesting for them.

And there are only 3 of us. One is selling. One is explaining. One is teaching. No coffee break.

Day 4 – Sunday, at different times. Prototypes.

Before Essen I scheduled meetings with various authors for Sunday. I was going to play prototypes and see if there was something interesting out there.

On Sunday I was going to have free time.

The situation, however, is very different. Our stand is crowded. We are selling *Robinson*, we are demoing *Robinson*, we have our hands full.

There is no chance to play prototypes. I have to apologize to the authors who had a meeting with me. I have no chance to play. I feel awful. I feel guilty. In fact I am guilty. I should feel awful.

I promise them I will play these prototypes as soon as I am back in Poland.

Day 4 – Sunday, 04:00 PM. Fatality.

I am extremely tired. We have no shifts for the demo table. Piechu sells, Scorn teaches, I have the demo table. I feel like a Czech android – the whole day I repeat the same sentences...

I have moments of weakness. People come to the table and wait for an explanation and I have no strength to go over to them and explain the game. They walk away after checking out the components of the game. I feel guilty. But I am terribly tired.

At some point another group of three people comes to the table. I take a deep breath. I look at them. And finally I walk over to the table. I am pissed off with myself and my weakness. I mentally motivate myself. I promise myself to never ever give up. And I start again: 'Robinson is a cooperative game. You are castaways on a deserted island and your goal is to survive. There are 6 different scenarios in the game and I will talk about them later on...'

I do my best. I find every little bit, every single piece of passion I have left and I use it.

From among those 3 people that listened to me, all three decided to buy *Robinson*. And what is more, one gamer who was just walking by and saw that they were very excited after my presentation and that they all bought the game... Well, he decided to buy the game too.

Three people listened. Four boxes of *Robinson* sold.

I am very tired. But I am back in action.

Day 4 – Sunday, 06:00 PM. The End.

At 6:00 PM the lights dim. Essen 2012 is over with. Whistles and applause fill the hall. Every publisher here is extremely tired. Every publisher here is happy that this is the end. This has been a tradition for a few years now. The lights dim, and the hall fills with whistles and applause.

This is for a short moment only. Then we have to go to work. Every publisher here has to clean their stand.

All games that have not been sold have to be packed back into boxes, then onto pallets, and finally onto trucks.

All games that have been sold to distributors need to be packed onto pallets and moved to their stands. All furniture, banners, and everything else that remains has to be packed into boxes and put onto trucks.

I think that if I did a poll right here and asked you how much time you think we would need to do all of this, no one would know the right answer. Let me show you...

It's 07:00 PM (you are probably taking a shower after a great fair). This is the first hour of moving heavy boxes for us...

It's 08:00 PM (you are probably at home already eating dinner). We are packing games.

It's 09:00 PM (you are tired after the fair, but you are very excited and you are unpacking games you bought). We are packing games. Still.

It's 10:00 PM (you have checked all the games you bought. You search the internet for news after Essen). We are packing games. We dream about lunch. We had no time for lunch today.

It's 11:00 PM (you are tired. You go to sleep). We are packing games. It's been 15 hours since we left our hotel. We dream about something to eat. Anything.

It's 11:30 PM. Yes, we are still there working...

It is hard to believe, but this is really true – when I reached our car in the Essen parking garage, it was exactly 00:01 AM. A very symbolic moment. After all these days of work during the fair we needed to find the strength to pack all these boxes of games for another 6 hours. Without a break.

We reached our hotel at 00:40. It would have been 00:20, but I was so tired while driving that I got lost in Essen. At 01:00 AM we ate a small meal – call it lunch. At 08:00 AM we started our drive back to Poland...

That, my friends, is Essen behind the scenes. I hope you enjoyed this ride...

WHY I HATE TOM VASEL ;)

[disclaimer: today I was going to post the final part of my report from Essen, but in the meantime Tom finished his Top 100 and I really needed to celebrate this and say something to Tom]

You know me much better than you knew me a few months ago. These days you know that I can talk about my games. You know that I really can show my passion. You know that I talk with a 100% belief in my games. And this belief is my strongest weapon. My weapon. The Weapon.

Tom Vasel can speak with a passion too. Tom can speak in such a way that we gamers are often defenseless. He uses the exact same weapon I am using. And damn, he is good at it too.

When you let me talk about *Robinson*, you will lose €45. I will make you buy the game. I open my mouth and you lose €45. When Tom talks about *Nothing Personal*, I lose $60 and $20 for shipping. And you know, I am from Poland. $80 for us is 16% of an average monthly salary in Poland. 16% of an average salary in the US is... It's like you'd pay $560 for *Nothing Personal*. Quite a price, right?

Yes, Tom is good...

But this is not why I hate him. I use my weapon on innocent gamers. Tom does it too. It is a fair trade.

But... [there is always 'a but', right?]

Tom makes his Top 100 videos.

He talks about 100 games other than *Nothing Personal*.

He talks about them with the same passion. He talks with the same fire in his eyes. He talks with the same belief – he believes that the game he is describing right now is for sure the best game on the planet. He uses The Weapon again.

This is not fair anymore. A few days ago he convinced me to buy *Star Trek Fleet Captains*. Guys, I hate Star Trek. I really hate this movie. Star Trek sucks! And still, I decided to buy the game...

I cannot buy all of those 100 games. I simply can't...

And you know, there are games on Tom's list I don't like. I played them and I think they suck. This is a moment of relief. 'Ha!' I think to myself when Tom talks about a game I don't like. 'We like different games! I shouldn't trust him! He knows nothing about good games! His recommendations suck. Ha!'

I am safe. I have neutralized The Weapon.

10 seconds later Tom starts to describe another game. A game I don't know. And again I start to trust him. Again I believe that this is the most awesome game on the planet. Again he uses The Weapon.

He uses The Weapon against me! Against The Weapon Master!

Stop it, Tom. Stop it now!

How I didn't win Spiel des Jahres

STRONGHOLD

PRET-A-PORTER

CONVOY

Nie może nigdy przejść do innej lokacji

SNIPER
ALL ROBOTS AND TREATED AS IF THEY HAD BLANK TXT on card

RADIO...

Nowy Jork

DESPERACKA OBRONA

JUGGERNAUT

BATTLE

POLE MINOWE
PUT IN EMPTY CITY. KILL FIRST ★ THAT APPEAR THERE. REMOVE "PM" FROM PLAY

BUNKIER

ŁOWCA

Opponent discard a card

RADIOSTACJA

KIERUNEK WIN... TAKE A CARD

NIE POTRZE...

STACJA NAPRAWCZA

② ROBOT

AFTER EVERY BATTLE ... THIS CITY, ... 1 CARD FROM ...RD & SHUFFLE ... DECK

Kills bu...

KASPAROV

USE skill of any ROBOT AGAIN

① BIEGACZ

PO UPADKU LOKACJI BIEGNIE DO AOACIENT CITY

LINIA UMOCN...

+3 : + ↻

+2 : ➡

+1 : NO EFFECT

0 : NO EFFECT

−1 : NO EFFECT

−2 : + ☑

−3 : +Thread action more
    → every round

−4 : • No Rerolls
    • DISCARD ALL rerolls
    • DON'T earn rerolls

ROBINSON CRUSOE

HOW TO SPEND A WEEKEND
AT A GAME CONVENTION
AND NOT PLAY A SINGLE GAME...

I met Silent a few years ago. He came to the 'Pawn' convention that I have been organizing in Gliwice since 2006. He was like many gamers who attend a con – he had a bag full of games, had a passion in his eyes and was able to play games for two days without taking even a 5 minute break.

After 'Pawn' he joined our gaming club. He lived in a different city, but for a man with a passion this is not a problem. He came to Gliwice every single week.

Another edition of 'Pawn' was coming. Silent came to me and said: 'I will help. I won't play. I will explain games to new gamers.'

We formed Team Orange. The most devoted members of our gaming club. During 'Pawn' Team Orange didn't play a single game. Two days of gaming and they didn't play even one single game. They were helping other players. They were explaining the rules. For the entire weekend.

That was incredible. At the end of the convention I asked them to come to the stage. And then the whole room burst into applause.

Now, six years later, this is the tradition. Every Pawn is supported by Team Orange. These Die Hard Gamers who decide to spend their weekend at a game convention and yet don't get to play a single game...

Every single Pawn, at the end of the convention, I invite them onto the stage, and every single time there is one full minute of amazing applause. Four hundred people clapping their hands to say 'Thank you'.

Goose-bumps...

'It's worth it.' Silent once told me. It's worth explaining rules for two days in a row. To be there on the stage at that very moment, and to see those 400 people in the room saying 'Thank you'. This is a magic moment.

***

Silent was a member of the first squad in Team Orange. This was six years ago. This weekend we will be doing the XIX edition of Pawn. Quite close to a nice anniversary. Six years passed like a dream.

Silent can no longer afford to be a member of our gaming club. He has a new job. He lives in another city. He is married. Years have passed.

He has no time for playing games like he used to when he was 24. Life has finally caught up with him and holds him in her tight grasp.

And yet...

I met Silent two weeks ago on a football pitch. 'We are doing a new edition of Pawn, you know,' I said.

'Nice. When?'

'In two weeks,' I said.

'Do you need help?' he asked.

'What do you think?... But, well, I know this is harder every time...'

'I have never turned you down, have I?' he said.

'Not once...'

'I will be there. I am Team Orange. This will never change.'

We shake hands. Two friends ready to go to the ends of the earth for each other.

***

The first Pawn was in 2006. Since then about 20 new conventions have appeared in Poland. Pawn was the first board game convention in Poland. Team Orange was the first supporters group. We all started that. Now you have Team Yellow in Gdansk, Team Blue in Wroclaw; you have such teams at every single board game convention in Poland.

And Poland is not an island.

There are conventions all over the world. There are people like Silent working hard to help you gamers all over the world. People who don't play, but help. For the whole damn weekend.

Silent, I thank you.

Team Orange, I thank you.

All teams and all supporters all around the world, I thank you.

You guys do an amazing job. I salute you.

Stretch goals
content

Stretch goals content content

STRETCH GOALS
CONTENT

KICK
STARTER
.COM

STRETCH GOALS
CONTENT

STRETCH GOALS CONTENT

STRETCH GOALS CONTENT

IGNACY TRZEWICZEK

NEUROSHIMA HEX

by Ignacy Trzewiczek

Neuroshima Hex is Portal's best-selling product. It was our first game to reach the Top 100 in the BGG ranking, our first game to be licensed and published in the US and then in France, Italy, Russia, and many other countries, our first game that was ported to iOS, giving us thousands of new players. For us, for Portal Games it all began with this one amazing board game.

Not too many of you probably know that the beginning of this great adventure was considerably less glorious.

***

It's spring 2003. I have just designed the card game *Zombiaki*, we've just published the RPG *Neuroshima* and in our free time we play *Kingdoms*, *Unexploded Cow*, and *Falling*. It is way before we discover *The Settlers of Catan* and the world of modern board games. Ancient times.

One day Michał Oracz brings a prototype to our office. You place units on a board, you can't move them, but the units have abilities. It looks like *Chess*, but without any movement. It's boring as hell. After one play I tell Michał I don't like it. He takes it back. I forget about it.

We get back to playing other games, such as *Light Speed, Cave Troll, Drakon,* and *Citadels...*

***

I get divorced. Every day I go to work and basically do nothing. I am in a vegetative state. Months pass, and Portal Games is in a very bad state. The company needs its boss back. But I am a wreck.

Finally I realize that either I immediately get back on my feet, or else Portal will die. I need to reset my brain. I decide to take one week vacation. I go to the countryside. No internet, no TV, just books and my laptop so I can write some stuff. A new beginning.

I remember the exact date – it is May 25, 2005. This day is etched in the history of football. AC Milan is playing against Liverpool in the Champions League final. It will be one of the most amazing football matches in history. I don't get to watch it because there is no TV there, in the countryside.

But back to board games.

That very day, the day when Liverpool won the Champions League, I got a message from Michał Oracz. It was about 6 or 7 PM. It said: 'We are still in the office. We are playing my game. It works amazingly well. Ignacy, you have to see this!'

On this day, May 25, 2005, *Neuroshima Hex* was born.

***

During the months previous to this day, Michał had been playing different games and improving his prototype at home. I didn't know this. He had been working on it without telling me. He took the draw rule from *Zombiaki*. He took the initiative rule from *Light Speed*. He took the scoring (battle!) mechanism from *Cave Troll*. He had been playing games and searching for elements that would make his prototype finally work.

On May 25, 2005 he was ready. Everything just clicked and fell into place.

***

We printed 1500 copies. I was very optimistic about the game as I really liked it. We sold 100. Yes, one hundred. We were left with 1400 copies. It was a disaster. This was 2005, the game market in Poland didn't exist yet, no one was interested in tactical board games. Everybody was playing either RPGs or M:tG and didn't give a shit about board games. In our office we had piles of boxes, everywhere. No one was buying the game. We were terrified.

Recently Michał Oracz told me how he remembered the devastated feeling he had during that time – every day when he entered the office and saw all those boxes, he thought to himself: 'God, I killed Portal. We won't survive this. What have I done?'

***

We needed to act or we were going to go down. I needed money. I could not afford having 1000+ boxes in my office. I made a desperate move.

We opened 300 boxes. We removed two armies from the box. We literally reduced the size of the game. And we sent a notice out to all the games stores that we had a new product. It was called *Neuroshima Hex Light*, it was a game for 2 players, and its MSRP was half that of the base game. Basically we were putting on a sale, but I was too proud to call it that.

Within a month we had sold all the copies of the light version we had made. In four weeks 300 copies of *Neuroshima Hex Light* found their owners. These 300 players played the game, and they recommended the game to everybody around. Believe it or not, now the base game began to sell too. Indeed, it began to sell like hot pies.

A mere 8 weeks later there wasn't a single copy of *Neuroshima Hex* left in our office. Just like that.

***

Practically overnight, *Neuroshima Hex* turned into a huge success. We earned a lot of money. We did a reprint. We went to Essen. You know the rest of the story. But, you know, when I look back at the beginning, when I see all those boxes in our office and literally no sales...

We were so damn close to bankruptcy. So close. It's a thin line between failure and success.

Life is a tricky bitch.

THE VOYAGE OF THE BEAGLE

by Ignacy Trzewiczek

It was a trap. From the very beginning it was a well prepared and well laid trap. Robert Masson was the hunter. I was the prey.

The trap is set
Robert created a team of players who wanted to design fan made scenarios. He collected a number of different ideas for the theme and he opened a poll. The theme that Robert suggested himself and loved the most, won. Luck? I don't think so...

Robert and his fellow testers began to work and within a few weeks they were ready to introduce us to their work. The Naturalist. A scenario about Charles Darwin. It was uploaded on BGG as a free mini expansion for *Robinson Crusoe*.

I really liked the idea for this scenario. I was happy that some fans had made content for my game and I was happy that this content was very good. I was kind of proud. I announced The Day of Robinson and I managed to have numerous people play this scenario simultaneously all around the world on this particular day, May 11, 2013. It was great fun.

The bait

Right after this event Robert contacted me and said that he and Marion, his most trusted tester had a small surprise for me. They had designed a second scenario, the sequel to The Naturalist scenario. And if I'd like to take a look at it.

I should have seen what was going to happen next. Well, I told him I'd love to take a look at their work.

They sent me the scenario. I really liked the idea of scenarios that are linked by one storyline.

Yeah, I know. I'd swallowed the bait like a fuckin' pelican.

I asked Robert if he had any more ideas to develop this story into an entire campaign. Robert answered that in fact he had ideas for two more scenarios about Charles Darwin.

The trap worked - I decided that I would publish it as an official expansion.

Houston, we have a...

The problem I discovered soon after I received all the files from Robert was that it looked like he hadn't played *Robinson* as much as I had. He had very interesting ideas. But many, I mean, *many* of them just didn't work in actual game play. They looked brilliant on paper, but not that brilliant when you saw them in action on the board.

At the end of June I received four scenarios. Each of them had some unique ideas and a really interesting theme. Each of them needed to be redesigned from scratch. They didn't work the way Robert had thought they would work. I was in trouble. We had no time at all. It was damn late.

No vacation this year

July was hell. I was on vacation with my family, and I spent the entire vacation playing *Robinson*. Merry was pissed off. The kids were not happy either. I had the game board for *Robinson* and all the scenarios set up on my table in our hotel room. I was totally sick of the game and I really didn't want to play it. When I signed *The Voyage of the Beagle* with Robert, I thought it would be a piece of cake – I was ready to publish an expansion, print it and earn a hell of a lot of money.

Well, it was July, I was stuck in Hungary playing *Robinson* all day long and it was far from being the stroll in the park that I had anticipated. It was hell.

Hell strikes back

When I got back to Poland, I called my most trusted testers and I welcomed them to hell. Five or six test games every single day, day after day, testing this campaign over and over. They knew they couldn't fail me, so they came to our office day after day, sat there all day long, playing this fucking *Robinson*. We hated the game.

There was one positive thing, one thing that kept us alive – this material Robert had created was very good. We were tired. We were pissed off. We were short of time, but above all, we knew – this is damn good. Damn good. It would be an amazing expansion when we were done with it.

In the meantime, when I was making some last tweaks to the rules, Robert was working on the rulebook and the scenario sheets. I put him through hell too. He worked day and night, correcting materials over and over. I screwed up his August as much as he screwed up my July. We were all complaining like hell, but we kept working as hard as we could.

[I have this image of Marek in my head. This is the last day of testing. He is the last man standing. He still has strength to play test. Still on duty. Still trying to find the right balance in the scenarios. An amazing job he did. You'll find his photo on page 156.]

Happy end

The Voyage of the Beagle was released at Essen 2013. It was a crazy ride, with Robert in the US, Marion testing scenarios in Germany, with an army of testers from all over the place, and with me and my team in Poland.

If I had known how hard it would be, I'd probably not have signed *The Voyage of the Beagle*. Fortunately, it was a well laid trap. I signed it and then the ride began.

The good news? *The Voyage of the Beagle* has a 8.89 rating on BGG and is an extraordinary product we are all super proud of. This is an exceptional expansion; I can tell you this without false modesty. We did something amazing.

The bad news? Merry has told me she won't go on vacation with me anymore. The summer of 2013 and *The Voyage of the Beagle* were too much for her.

ABOUT TESTING... AGAIN

by Ignacy Trzewiczek

That day we were testing *Cannibal Island* for *Robinson Crusoe*. I had Marek and Maciek in our office. Marek is one of my most trusted testers. Maciek was new. He didn't know what was coming...

They played once and lost. They played again and lost terribly. Maciek looked at me with his eyes saying something like: 'I hope that next time I am here, this scenario will be balanced,' but Marek didn't stop for even a second. He began to set up the game again. 'We play again!' he ordered. So they played again. They lost. Marek was pissed off. 'I'll beat this motherfucker!' he said and again began to set up. 'I'll have to go now,' said Maciek, and escaped from the office...

***

As I have written in so many articles, testing is not fun. Testing is not hanging around with friends and playing games. Testing is not meeting once a week and playing a game with beer and pretzels.

Testing is painstaking work. It is playing a game over and over, playing three, four games in a row, playing it again and again. Right after you finish a game you take a 3-minute break to make a coffee and you set it up again, and then again. Testing is making you hate the game. None of my *Robinson Crusoe* testers played the game when it was finally released. They all hate the game. The better work we do, the more difficult it is for us when we see the final product.

It is really hard to find the right way to thank all the people who are behind the author. It's his name on the box, it's him getting awards, it's him getting royalties. The testers? Their names in small font at the end of the rulebook. Is there anybody who reads that? And even so, even if somebody reads that, do you really know how much work it was to playtest a game? The list of testers is not a list of buddies who played the prototype and drank beer. This is a list of people who were killing themselves in order to make this game amazing.

I have this photo of Marek. It is the last day of testing *Voyage of the Beagle* (you can read about it in one of the other articles). All the testers stopped answering my phones. All the testers disappeared. Even my most trusted people had had enough. It was too much, even for them. I was left alone.

Marek showed up. He didn't give up. He came again, tired but ready to play this damn campaign again. I looked at him sitting in our office, testing the 4-player variant. He looked like the hero from the movie 13th Warrior. The last man standing.

I owe him this. Thank you Marek. And a great big thank you to all testers who have supported me for all these years.

IMPERIAL SETTLERS

by Ignacy Trzewiczek

On August 29, 2012 I posted an article on BGG entitled 'Why I needed three years to discover Frozen City'. It described the process of me developing an expansion for *51ˢᵗ State* and *The New Era* and the *Winter* expansion. I showed how these expansions made the base game better. In the last paragraph of this article I wrote:

'Every year, when I finish my new design I am 100% sure that this is a perfect game. I see no flaws. I see no points where it could be improved. I see it as a brilliant piece of work.

And year after year I learn something new. Every year I discover new stuff. Every year it turns out that I can do better.

Today I am happy to announce – without false modesty – that Winter is a perfect card game.

But to be honest I have a hunch I may want to change this statement next year...'

It's February 6, 2014, and I have news for you. *Winter* is not a perfect card game.

***

Some of the first illustrations from the game.

It began in 2013. We were discussing our future plans and I had this crazy idea – let's try to make *51st State* with a fantasy theme. A few months earlier I created a small game for my kids at home and it played really smoothly. I changed scrap/incorporation to wood/building, I changed gun/invade to gold/buy. I changed fuel/deal to food/deal. The kids really liked the idea of building a fantasy settlement and played it a number of times. We decided at Portal that it was worth a shot and I would create a full prototype for testing.

Coincidentally, around the same time I was at some convention and I was asked to run a demo for *51st State*. For all of you who know the game, this will not come as a surprise – this game is unexplainable. Running a demo at a convention is like torture. So many rules. So many exceptions. So many icons. It was an ordeal.

In fact, it was the best that could happen. I got home with a very strong resolution. I am not retheming *51st State*. I am redesigning it. And so the journey began.

***

It took me much more time than I had initially expected. It turned out that in fact I was designing a brand new game. I was cutting and cutting and cutting the rules for *51st State* for such a long time that in the end there was nearly nothing left. And even though it is hard to believe, nothing changed.

The fun remained.

Different strategies could be used to win the game.

Merry loves the game.

And what is most important, I can explain the rules in less than 5 minutes now.

***

This is part of the job of being a game designer. This is part of the job and I really hate it. When it's done, it's done. You can't do anything about it anymore. It goes to print, it goes to game stores, it goes to gamers and ends up on their tables.

I can't send you a free update. You can't download new content from my website.

And in fact, you don't even want to hear that I have an update! You don't want to hear that right after I published the game, I got this brilliant new idea and if I could only postpone production, the game would be better. You don't want to know this, do you? You don't want to have the feeling that this game could have been better if only the designer had had an additional six months...

The case is, every designer has it with every damn game. We are creators. We have strange, twisted minds that work all the time and create something new. We get better, we learn, we play new games, we become more experienced. And we think about our games over and over.

That is why *The New Era* is better than *51st State*, and that is why *Winter* is better than *The New Era*, and that is why *Imperial Settlers* is better than *Winter*... That is how it works. We improve all the time.

***

I can't look at my games. I see only mistakes. I see only things I would design better this time. This is a part of my job that really sucks. I hate my published games...

POSITIVE VIBRATIONS

by Ignacy Trzewiczek

I remember it exactly – we were driving back to our hotel in Modena with Martin Wallace. Tired but happy after a long day at the PLAY Modena Fair. At some point Martin said something like: 'There are many nice people working in the gaming industry. Perhaps it is because it is still a small industry and there is no real money here. Everybody is kind and honest.'

I can confirm this. Absolutely most of the people in our industry are super cool. I have the honor to have here in this book many amazing people who work in the gaming industry, I have written about them in the bio section. And this is just the tip of the iceberg...

Let's start with the BGG team, people who every single year have to struggle with the pronunciation of my name when recording videos from Essen. I have to say, all of them – Aldi, Chad, Katherine, John and the rest of the team are fully dedicated to their passion. Recording all of those videos about games is a huge amount of work. They have to listen to designers talk about their games for five days in a row. Let's face it – this is hardcore. I would die after a few hours.

And they do it for five days. Smiling, energized, doing their best to provide you with the best material directly from the convention.

The same with authors; I have had only positive experiences. Bruno Faidutti was super supportive of me when I was an unknown author from Poland. Friedemann Friese has a great sense of humor. Michiel Hendriks is super smart and super kind, and Martin Wallace the same – a kind and humble person...

Other people in our hobby? Rahdo with his super energy, and Vasel with his quest to review every single game out there, and Joel Eddy, Zee Garcia, and Sam Healey, who thinks that X-Wing is a 3 player game. Then there's Rodney from Watch It Played, and the guys who do all those cool podcasts about games... They are all super cool people. I mean, every single time I meet another person who is part of our hobby and contributes to it somehow, it is the same – passionate gamers, friendly people.

It is true, the gaming industry is not that big. There is no real money in it, as they say. I am quite a successful author and publisher, but I don't have a PS4, I don't have the latest iPad, I don't have a fancy car. I make average money, just enough to make a living.

The truth is I don't give a shit about real money.

I am surrounded by people whom I love and respect. And that is why I would never consider changing to a different industry. The gaming industry is where it's at, for me.

TWENTY YEARS WITH THE WITCHER

by Ignacy Trzewiczek

The photo you see here shows one of the books in my house. I bought it 20 years ago, at Polcon '93. As a seventeen year old kid with a great potential to become a true nerd, I went to Polcon, the largest SF convention in Poland. It was an amazing time. I sat in meetings with authors, I talked with other nerds, I watched SF movies on pirated VHS tapes. I was in paradise.

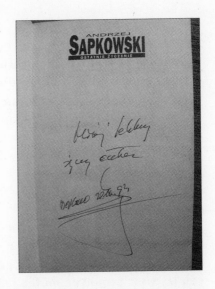

Every day, my head down as I was pretty shy, I stood in line for autographs of my favorite writers. This one above, the autograph of Andrzej Sapkowski, was the most valuable trophy among those that I brought home. Andrzej Sapkowski wrote *The Witcher*. Oh yes, I had a book signed by the Master! The year was 1993, and I had just turned 17...

***

My efforts to create a game in the world of The Witcher began around the beginning of 2011. Taking into account the number of successful board games that I had in my CV I thought that this was a good moment to take another step forward. I made an offer to CD Projekt Red. I wanted to design Witcher: The Board Game.

There were talks, negotiations, first sketches of the prototypes. There was little to no progress in the talks, and finally, after some time, eventually they collapsed.

I'm not a man who is easily discouraged. I used all my contacts to get the contact information of Andrzej Sapkowski himself! I made him an offer. Again, the exchange of e-mails, some explanations and presentations, but in the end, once again – things fell apart.

I thought it was the end...

***

At the beginning of 2012, I received an email from CD Projekt Red saying that they were ready to resume negotiations. The project took off. More visits to Warsaw, presentations, various versions of the prototypes, gaining confidence and looking for a solution that would satisfy everyone. We were looking for a game that would be as low as possible for entry for casual gamers and at the same time would offer more experienced players interesting choices and fun...

***

So this was the day. The bigwigs of CD Projekt Red, a conference room and me with the prototype. Great, huh? I'm a cocky guy, I really am, and I have a strong belief in my games, but at such moments, when you lay your prototype on the table, even a tough guy like myself feels his knees buckle.

I was shaking like a leaf.

They played. There was laughter, they were using the engines I had designed and I saw they were having fun. Finally, the game was over.

My heart was pounding like a drum. I saw that they had had a good time, I saw that everything worked, but still... I was terrified.

'It was great. I really felt like I was playing Dandelion!' says Adam. 'Excellent!'

Phew!

***

Into *The Witcher* I put 20 years of my passion for SF and fantasy. By giving CD Projekt Red the prototype of the game I summed up 20 years of my life - my trips to conventions, reading hundreds of SF books, subscriptions to SF and fantasy magazines, hours spent in the cinema... If all those hours spent on the fascination for SF were to ever return, this was the time.

They returned when I created a deck for Dandelion and I filled it with lovers and jealous husbands, unforeseen problems, surprise fights and mistakes...

They returned when I gave Geralt an incredible power in combat, possibilities that at first and even second glance seem totally unbalanced. Any player who gets Geralt in their hands smiles evilly, seeing how many options he has in melee combat...

They returned when all my love for dwarves concentrated itself in the rules for Yarpen. I gave him a bunch of dwarven companions and I turned them all into a merry company of tanks...

They returned when I let Triss, the sorceress, be a real wizard. I gave her an arsenal of spells, which allows her to feel that to be a magician means to be more than a human...

***

If in 1993 when I was heading back home from Polcon three witches would have met me on my way and prophesied my future, I would not have believed them. I was a teenager from a small town dreaming about writing a short story in a fantasy setting. My imagination at that time had no right to allow me to fly so high as to dream of the creation of an official game in the world created by my Master, Andrzej

Sapkowski, the same Sapkowski whose autograph I was carrying in my backpack as my greatest treasure.

And yet, now I'm the guy who has designed the official game for the world of *The Witcher.*

They say that sometimes dreams come true. Well, it seems that sometimes reality even surpasses dreams...

PORTAL FOUNDATION

by Ignacy Trzewiczek

When I was in high school I was a typical nerd. I was that guy you all know from sitcoms and movies. That scraggy kid with huge glasses playing D&D all day long. Yeah. That was me. Of course, I had no idea what I wanted to do with my life, I had no idea which college to choose, I just played games and had fun.

Yes, I know. It is a rather embarrassing story.

Anyway, at some point I had to choose. My father had a business that operated in the environmental sector doing some recycling stuff and since I am the firstborn son it seemed quite natural that I should study something dedicated to the environment so I would be able to take over my father's firm when I grew up.

So I went to college to study how to protect our planet.

I am a smart guy, so even though I didn't give a shit about the lectures or the classes, and spent all day playing games, I managed to do quite well in the first year. And in the second year. And even in the third year of college. It was getting more and more ridiculous. Every month it seemed to me to be more and more like I was studying Chinese or the economy of Norway. I had no idea what the classes were all about. Somehow, however, I was passing exams one after another.

Lecturers knew I had no idea what I was doing there, but well, I was this funny guy. And every class needs one, right?

Yes, I know. This story keeps getting more and more embarrassing.

***

At some point I really needed money. I could take a job on the side, earn a small amount of cash, but I was a nerd, so I got this crazy idea, an idea that can be born only in a nerd's head. The idea was: 'I will write an RPG scenario, and then I will send it to an RPG magazine, and I will earn money and fame.'

It was fucking stupid, but there was nobody to tell me that. So I wrote the scenario, sent it up, and waited for an answer.

And that's where my embarrassing story changes into a fairytale: the magazine replied.

They published the scenario. They paid me. The scenario was chosen by readers as the best article published in that issue. The magazine told me they wanted more.

I wrote more. They published that too. They paid me. The readers voted. Every single piece of material that I sent them was popular with the readers. People loved to read my RPG stuff. That was so awesome.

The fourth year of my college began. I still had no idea what I was doing there. I still passed my exams, one after the other. I didn't have a clue what I was passing, but with a lot of help from my fellow students I crawled forward. Two years left...

***

I passed all the exams during my fourth year of college. One year left.

I knew it didn't make any sense. I was studying stuff I was totally not interested in. I was heading into a direction that led me to think: 'You will spend your life doing recycling.' Week after week I was getting closer to becoming my father's right hand and running his business with him. There was no more time for jokes. This was the moment that would define my entire life.

So I sat down with my dad and I told him that I was going to drop out of college. I told him I wasn't going to help him with his firm.

I told him that I was going to start my own small company, that I was going to publish an RPG magazine.

You can imagine his reaction. It was like my father had been hit by a truck. This is not the kind of news you want to hear from your firstborn. I know. Until this day I can't believe I told him this...

But my father did what fathers do. He accepted my decision. He gave me money to start my company. He wished me luck on my own path.

***

Every single day I wake up a happy person. I go to work with a smile on my face. I work all day long and I feel like I am just playing all day long.

This is because 15 years ago my father had the guts to accept me dropping out of college. This is because 15 years ago I had the guts to refuse a well-paid job as the vice president of my father's company and jumped into the unknown.

I wish all of you the same. Have guts. Follow your dreams.

Antoine Bauza

Antoine
Bauza

ANTOINE
BAUZA

ANTOINE BAUZA

ANTOINE BAUZA

Antoine
Bauza

ANTOINE
BAUZA

Ignacy about Antoine:

It's April 2010 and I am in France at Bruno Faidutti's Gathering of Friends. I heard about an interesting prototype that Antoine had with him, so one evening I asked him if I might play it. Antoine agreed. It was late and Merry said she was tired and preferred not to play, so she ended up going to bed while I stayed with Antoine and two other players to play. It was a card game, and the rules were simple, the game played quickly and in less than an hour we were done. I won.

I went to bed, and Merry woke up and asked how I liked the game. 'It was fun,' I said, 'but I can do better.'

I said that, because I was working on the prototype for *51ˢᵗ State* at that moment and I was pretty sure my game would be mind-blowing.

A few months later *51ˢᵗ State* was released and it was a blast indeed. I received the *Golden Geek Best Card Game Nominee, JoTa Best Card Game Nominee* and the *G@mebox Award* at Boardgame.de.

The prototype I was playing that evening was *7 Wonders*. It was released a few months later. And in fact, it was a blast too. It received the *Meeples' Choice Award, Tric Trac d'Or, Tric Trac Nominee, As d'Or - Jeu de l'Année Nominee, As d'Or - Jeu de l'Année Prix du Jury Winner, Deutscher Spiele Preis Best Family/Adult Game Winner, Fairplay À la carte Winner, Golden Geek Best Board Game Artwork/Presentation Nominee, Golden Geek Best Card Game Nominee, Golden Geek Best Card Game Winner, Golden Geek Best Family Board Game Nominee, Golden Geek Best Family Board Game Winner, Golden Geek Best Innovative Board Game Nominee, Golden Geek Best Party Board Game Nominee, Golden Geek Best Strategy Board Game Nominee, Gouden Ludo Nominee, Gouden Ludo Winner, Gra Roku Game of the Year Nominee, Guldbrikken Best Adult Game Nominee, Guldbrikken Best Adult Game Winner, Hra roku Nominee, Hra roku Winner, International Gamers Award - General Strategy: Multi-player Winner, International Gamers Awards - General Strategy; Multi-player Nominee, Japan Boardgame Prize Voters' Selection Nominee, Japan Boardgame Prize Voters' Selection Winner, JoTa Best Artwork Critic Award, JoTa Best Artwork Nominee, JoTa Best Card Game Audience Award, JoTa Best Card Game Critic Award, JoTa Best Card Game Nominee, JoTa Best Light Board Game Audience Award, JoTa Best Light Board Game Critic Award, JoTa Best Light Board Game Nominee, Juego del Año Finalist, Juego del Año Tico Nominee, Juego del Año Tico Winner, Lucca Games Best Boardgame*

BOARDGAMES THAT TELL STORIES

Nominee, Lucca Games Best Boardgame Winner, Lys Passioné Finalist, Lys Passioné Winner, Nederlandse Spellenprijs Nominee, Spiel des Jahres Kennerspiel des Jahres Winner, Spiel des Jahres Kennerspiel Game of the Year Nominee, Vuoden Peli Adult Game of the Year Nominee, Vuoden Peli Adult Game of the Year Winner, Boardgames Australia Awards Best International Game Nominee, Ludoteca Ideale Winner, Hungarian Board Game Award Nominee.

Yeah. I can-do-better-my-ass.

Antoine is a top notch designer. From *Ghost Stories* to *7 Wonders*, from *Tokaido* to *Rampage*, his games are always about fun, they are entertaining and are aimed directly at gamers' hearts. What a brilliant designer. For this book Antoine tells the story of *Hanabi*, one of Merry's favorite games.

IGNACY TRZEWICZEK

Follow him on twitter: @Toinito
Subscribe to: http://www.antoinebauza.fr/

HANABI, AN INCREDIBLE STORY!

by Antoine Bauza

Hanabi, a small, cooperative and very peculiar card game, won the Spiel des Jahres 2013, the most prestigious award in the board gaming community. During the press conference that followed the ceremony, a journalist asked me if *Hanabi* was my first game and, as the interview continued, he seemed to believe that I had woken up one bright, sunny morning, designed *Hanabi* that day and that, perhaps the very next day, the game won the biggest award in the industry.

I love it when people express their vision of a creative activity and how it often happens to be very straightforward in their mind: you have a brilliant idea. You make the game. Get a publisher. Achieve success. Done. Well, it turns out that it was not so simple, and I struggled a lot with those colored powders before the big fireworks... worked! This is the incredible story of a little game called *Hanabi.*

Caravelle (2009)
Though it was released onto the market in 2010, this card game is actually one of my earliest designs, dating back to the time when I was still writing roleplaying games, around 2005. In the beginning there was one game, perhaps my first completed game project,

a competitive push-your-luck game called *Ikebana*. This game worked well, and I had the graphic design done by my wife, so it was a nice, good-looking little prototype. I met a young publisher of roleplaying games, Caravelle, at a gaming convention and I introduced my game to him, well, to her actually. She liked it and she was about to publish a first card game herself. So *Ikebana* could be their second card game publication. Nice, let's do this!

Caravelle was a very small publisher with limited resources and therefore little visibility. When I got home, I started to look for a way to distinguish my card game from the dozens of other small games already available on the market. My components were fairly standard (55 numbered cards and a handful of chips), so I thought I might be able to design a second game with them. If Caravelle released a little box with two games in it, it would allow it to (perhaps) stand out from the competition. It seemed like an interesting idea and it was also an interesting style exercise. Sometime later, I presented *Hanabi* to Caravelle. A second game, always competitive and always about combinations, but with a different mechanism. The idea was warmly welcomed: *Hanabi & Ikebana*, two colorful games sharing a nice Japanese theme. All in the same little box...

Unfortunately, Caravelle closed before the release of the game (and just after the release of *Nains & Jardins*, my last contribution to roleplaying games). The project therefore lay dormant for several months, the time it took for me to get back the rights to the game... and to find another publisher.

XII Singes (2010)

XII Singes is another small publisher, and also a publisher of roleplaying games, who showed interest a year later. XII Singes had plans to add some small card games to their collection of roleplaying books. *Hanabi & Ikebana* fit perfectly. They introduced the prototype to their gaming circle and Franck, the CEO, came back to me with the following observation: 'We like it, but both games are too similar in their mechanisms. If we want to claim there are two games in one box, the difference between the two mechanisms will need to be greater. Can you think this through?' So I did...

Sometimes when I am stuck in the design process, I lay out the prototype on a large, empty table (a clean one if possible...) and I handle the components, manipulating them while I think. It is while I was going through this little ritual that I came to take a few cards in my hand, holding them backwards, the 'good side' outward. I really loved the idea, I just had to find a mechanism to go with it. (Sounds easy, huh? Well, it's not.) I imagined a game in which each player held his hand of cards backwards and tried to reconstruct pairs of the same value by taking a card from an opponent's hand and a map from their own hand. To do this, the player would be entitled to request information about his hand from other players. Thus *Hanabi* was born, though it was a competitive game. The tests were inconclusive, but the principle of a hand of cards facing backwards was very well received by all play testers. Hmmm...

Back at my desk, I tried to come up with another mechanism... I was there, my head in my hands, grinding my teeth ... when my wife came in and saw me scowling at my cards. With what only could be a wife's insight, she said: 'Why don't you do a cooperative game? You like those so much, right?' ...??? ... Damn! Those words blew my mind! Why had I not thought of that? Of course I had to do a cooperative game, the hand of cards facing backwards would work very well! Players play together, but they are not aware of their own hand of cards. They need to obtain information in order to play the right card at the right time with the aim to reconstruct the 5 colored suits, the fireworks. In other words: Playing a card, Giving a hint, Discarding to get back information tokens. Simple enough. Back to the playtest, and it worked well this time! Back to XII Singes with my updated unique selling point: 'A competitive game and a cooperative game, all in one box.' How about that, players! I knew this time I had got it right... XII Singes thought so too... So *Hanabi & Ikebana* were published in 2010. 1000 copies were printed for the French market...

A word about the theme before going on with the timeline. Fireworks and floral composition were present in my first prototype and that never changed. *Hanabi & Ikebana* are abstract games indeed, but the thematic references clearly express the duality of two games sharing the same components (the Japanese ideogram 'flower' is found in the words *fireworks* – Hana/Bana – *and floral composition*). The graphic design was done by my wife and based on traditional Japanese motifs. Whether at Caravelle or XII Singes, the artwork budget was not very high and this solution had the virtue of being economical and original. With hindsight, I realize that not everyone shares my sensitivity to these traditional designs, but selfishly, I do not care a bit! This was an opportunity to do something a little less conventional.

Cocktail Games (2011)

I don't exactly remember when I got Matthieu d'Epenoux, CEO of the French publisher Cocktail Games, to play the game, but Matthieu had a blast! He really loved the game. So I told him to contact XII Singes to find a way to export the game to the rest of the world. He did so. We discussed a new release of the game. It had to be in a metal box, because all games published by Cocktail Games are. Matthieu wanted to keep only *Hanabi* and get rid of its big brother *Ikebana*. I was a bit reluctant to do so due to the history of these two brothers, but it was the right solution. So finally I agreed, and that was that.

Cocktail Games worked on the game, changing the graphics, designing square cards as they always do. They sent me the files the day before they were supposed to go to the manufacturer... The problem was simple: I really disliked the graphics they had made. They just didn't match my idea of what the game should look like at all (and I'm very picky about the graphics of my games, I confess). So I convinced Matthieu to let me redo the artwork from scratch in less than 24 hours... Well, when I said 'let me' I in fact mean 'let my wife'... Honey? There is something I'd like to ask you... Do you have a couple of hours for me right now?

So, after a complete redesign of the artwork done in less than a day of labor, the Cocktail Games version was released. The first Cocktail Games print run sold out quickly. It allowed the game to reach a wider audience and to cross borders... The story continues...

Abacusspiele (2012)

Matthias Wagner from Abacusspiele contacted me after playing the game during Bruno Faidutti's Ludopathic Gathering in Spring 2012. Like Matthieu, he loved the game at first sight. Cocktail Games had the rights, so I was thinking that the game should be published in

Germany by HUCH! & Friends, the regular partner of Cocktail Games in this market. But in fact, HUCH! & Friends did not take the game despite the efforts of Cocktail Games. So, Matthias took a shot at it and Abacusspiele released the German version in October 2012.

Spiel des Jahres (2013)

May 2013, I was working on my computer (read 'wasting time on social network sites') when I discovered that *Hanabi* had been nominated for the famous German board game award Spiel des Jahres! Wow... That was a surprise! Amazing! The game was successful for sure, but a SdJ nomination, really? To tell the truth, I had always seen *Hanabi* as a lab experiment, and now the game was on the short list for the main award in the board game industry. Well, I thought, let's pack for Germany then...

Berlin, Monday July 8, a bright, sunny morning (ha, here is that bright, sunny morning at last, Mr. Journalist!). I took a flight from France with Matthieu d'Epenoux (Cocktail Games), Sébastien Celerin (XII Singes) and Philippe Maurin (Mr. Phal from Tric Trac). Here we are in the beautiful press conference room of a fancy hotel downtown. I missed the Kennerspiel des Jahres award for *7 Wonders*, back in 2011: I was stuck in South Korea. So it's my first time here. Many guests (mostly journalists and publishers) are wearing suits and I am among them in my usual casual outfit, trying not to stand out too much. It should be OK, as nobody really thinks that *Hanabi* could possibly win, right?

Did I believe *Hanabi* had a chance to win against *Augustus* (at this time, I hadn't heard much about *Qwixx*, which is a really good game that I have played a lot since...)? Well... not really, in fact. *Hanabi* is such a peculiar game: it's a card game, it's a cooperative game, it's a game in which players have to build their own ways of playing it, add their own communication rules, make it work... It's a long shot! I was thinking that the jury gave it a nomination to reward its originality. But give it the award, no...

You know the rest. *Hanabi* did win. As I told Tom Felber (president of the SdJ Jury) when he asked me how I felt: I was happy, of course. It was an important day in my career as a game designer, but, more than that, it was a very strong signal sent by the Jury to the whole industry: you can make special games, you can make coop games, you can make small games, and if they are great, they can win the award.

What Next? (2014...)

Abacusspiele has released a beautiful (but expensive) deluxe edition to celebrate the SdJ victory, and new countries have contacted *Cocktail Games* about importing the game. We expect to reach 1 million copies in 2014... Not bad for a game that started with a first run of 1000 'French only' copies, don't you think?

So, to answer that journalist's question, no, I didn't just wake up one bright, sunny morning, designed *Hanabi* during breakfast, play-tested it for lunch, and had it published in the afternoon. The story of *Hanabi* is a little more than just a perfect day...

Kulkmann   Frank Schulte

FRANK
SCHULTE

KULKMANN

KULKMANN

Frank
Schulte
Kulkmann

FRANK
SCHULTE

Ignacy about Frank:

I met Frank for the first time at Essen 2010. Portal Games was releasing *51ˢᵗ State* and right before the convention I was contacted by Frank. He was interested in playing *51ˢᵗ State*. I told my friends from Rebel that some reviewer had contacted me and asked whether they had ever heard about some guy called Kulkmann.

'Are you f... kidding?! He is one of the most respected reviewers in Germany. His site is one of the best visited sites during Essen. His reports and reviews are super important!'

'Wow. Didn't know that.'

So I arranged a meeting. Frank came. We sat down together, and I began to explain the rules, but he said: 'I know the rules. I have already read the rulebook. We can just play.' OK, that was something new. He played, he liked the game, and he awarded it on his website as the Essen Hit 2010.

Yeah. Very nice story, don't you think?

We have met up with Frank every Essen since then. He is the best prepared reviewer I have ever heard of. Months before Essen he reads rulebooks, learns about games, and then, during these crazy 4 days of gaming at Essen, he plays as many games as possible and writes reviews of them late into the night. Amazing work. Year after year.

He has a great wife, he is super kind, he is German, but his website is in English and... If you do happen to make it to Essen, find him and meet up with him! Or at least, follow his website!

Follow him on twitter: @Kulkmann
Subscribe to: http://boardgame.de

THE REVIEWER'S STORY

by Frank Schulte-Kulkmann

Theatre critics, tax inspectors, board game reviewers – all these groups have in common that they prey on other people's creativity, picking apart what has been assembled with care, hope and devotion...

Well, I hope that, in the end, board game designers do not hold such a bad opinion about people who write and publish reviews of their games, but nonetheless it's a fact that reviewers can be harsh and merciless when it comes to assessing the work and effort a designer has put into his game. In some cases criticism may be justified because a game comes with incomprehensible rules or – even worse – the game mechanics suffer from certain defects which have gone unnoticed during the development phase. However, more often than not board game designers are canny enough to give a wide berth to these obvious pitfalls. The reviewer then faces the task of evaluating a game based on its inherent qualities – an exercise which may prove quite a challenge since at the end of the day the review should be adequate and reconcile different aspects such as game mechanics, rules and the quality of all components.

You might ask yourself what this all has to do with 'Boardgames That Tell Stories'. As far as many gamers and board game designers alike are concerned, games and stories somehow belong together; hence a book looking at this topic from many different perspectives should sensibly include some input from a reviewer's perspective. Personally, having started reviewing games in 1996 (and belonging to two of the groups listed above), I feel fairly competent to comment on the link between games and stories from a reviewer's point of view. However, I do not claim that my opinions on this topic mirror the view generally accepted by a majority of game reviewers, and so I would just like to give you an idea of my own personal understanding of the connection between games and stories.

As already mentioned above, there are many different factors a game reviewer has to take into account when it comes to developing an opinion about a game. Firstly, the game mechanics need to be examined for their originality, their coherence and their elegance. Flaws in this category often prove disastrous since the game will lack a proper backbone, but, on the other hand, a game which scores high in this area still is not necessarily a smash hit. Different reviewers will certainly hold diverse opinions on this aspect; however, from my point of view, the game mechanics are to be considered a solid core around which other elements must be arranged in order to create a successful board game. Replay value, graphical design and – last but not least – the implementation of the background story are the most important of these additional elements, and only if all of them make for a harmonious whole a game will score top marks in my reviews.

As a matter of fact, the implementation of the background story is of special importance to me, because I appreciate and enjoy a game which is not limited to posing an interesting challenge due to its mechanics. Playing board games is a great pastime, and if the background story and game mechanics are nicely interwoven, the game has its own special charm because it appeals not only to the gamer's tactical skills, but also to his imagination. That's not to say each and every element of a game necessarily has to be linked to its own background story (though I still remember how Ignacy was able to come up with a story for every single card included in *51ˢᵗ State*); instead, what is important is that the general rhythm of a game and its background story are congruent. I would like to highlight Antoine Bauza's *7 Wonders* or Michael Menzel's *Legends of Andor* as two examples of a perfect fusion of game mechanics and background story. Both games have succeeded in fascinating gamers around the world for months and indeed years – a fact which I attribute to the game mechanics and the implementation of the background story alike. Both factors contribute to an exciting playing atmosphere, and it is exactly this atmosphere that will keep a game on the table for many gaming sessions to come.

At times, a coherent incorporation of the background story may even straighten out some minor flaws, because a thrilling and absorbing course of the game will help gamers turn a blind eye to minor drawbacks. Good examples are Ignacy's *Robinson Crusoe – Adventure on the Cursed Island* and *Luna Llena: Full Moon* by Servando Carballar. The rulebooks of both games are bulky and could have been structured a bit more clearly, but the quite enthralling background stories and playing atmosphere found in both games helped me to overcome this initial hurdle easily. Another example is *Empires of the Void* by Ryan Laukat. The rulebook included in the game's Kickstarter-edition left some questions unanswered. Those were answered later in an FAQ, while a print-and-play expansion published afterwards contained a set of further revised rules. This might certainly entice some reviewers to disapprove of a game, but in my view the game offered a refreshing new approach to the topic of galactic conquest because it cleverly avoided becoming just another time-consuming monster--game. With an emphasis on timing and a rather limited number of available actions, Ryan charmingly connected the background story to some new twists – for me, this was reason enough to award the game a good score in my review.

In some instances the persuasive implementation of a thrilling plot may even lead to me savoring a game that is simply driven by luck and chance. For example, I really enjoy playing *Zombicide* by Raphaël Guiton, Jean-Baptiste Lullien and Nicolas Raoult, despite the fact that this game is, in essence, a dice-driven board game adaptation of a first-person shooter.

On the other end of the spectrum you can find games where mechanics and background story are mashed up rather arbitrarily. Personally, I think it's quite unnerving if a game's background story is not reflected in its rules. At times, there is nothing more deceptive than a gorgeously illustrated box with a winsome blurb on the back

– only to leave you increasingly disappointed when everything turns out to be bare decoration if not camouflage of mediocre game mechanics. Under these circumstances I certainly prefer a purely abstract game such as Stefan Kiehl's *Moeraki-Kemu* or *Yōkaï no Mori* (a 'Shōgi' clone) by Madoka Kitao. Both of these games still tell a story, but it is evident that the players' main focus lies with the strategic conflicts carried out on the game board.

Of course, my view on the link between games and stories expressed here is rather subjective and certainly reflective of my own preferences; nevertheless, it is my firm belief that games and stories cannot truly be separated. In fact, a quick glance at various board game awards like the International Gamers Award, Deutscher Spiele Preis or Spiel des Jahres reveals that many of the former awardees feature not only outstanding game mechanics but also well-implemented background stories; thus, board games obviously profit from the incorporation of a well-chosen background.

In his blog Ignacy explains his design philosophy, which boils down to his belief that 'a good board game is one that tells a good story'. Of course, a good story alone does not reveal anything about the qualities of a game, but as a reviewer and as a gamer I am happy that many designers follow a similar approach, creating games which offer an all-encompassing playing experience!

Michał Oracz

Michał Oracz

MICHAŁ ORACZ

MICHAŁ ORACZ

MICHAŁ ORACZ

Michał Oracz

MICHAŁ ORACZ

Ignacy about Michał:
I could write a whole book about Michał. He has been my friend for nearly half my life, we have had amazing adventures together and if there is one person who has influenced my life most (except my family), it is Michał. If I hadn't met him years ago, my life would have looked very different from what it is now.

It was 1999. I had just founded Portal and we were going to publish bi-monthly magazines about RPG games. At one convention we met Tomasz Oracz, a Polish painter who was an amazing artist and happened to live in a city near us. After a convention we arranged to meet with him at his home to see all his paintings.

I went there, checked out the paintings (they were awesome!), talked about future cooperation and our plans. When I was leaving he said something like, 'My younger brother actually plays RPGs too. Perhaps you would like to meet him?'

I didn't really want to, actually. The younger brother sounded like a 12 year old kid who played D&D with his schoolmates. But I really wanted to have Tomasz on board and didn't want to offend him, so I said: 'Sure!'

That one 'Sure' changed my whole life.

It turned out that the younger brother was 25 years old, had been playing RPGs for ten years and knew about ten times more about games than me. This was the first person I had ever met who knew more about gaming than me. Quite something.

Michał Oracz is the smartest person I know. He works hard, he does amazing things and he has this super important construction in his head – he thinks big. He doesn't just design a game. He designs the best game there is. He doesn't care for less than best. That is why he keeps coming up with amazing stuff.

ON RESPECTING PLAYERS' INTELLIGENCE

by Michał Oracz

I've been designing puzzles for fifteen years now. Brain teasers about breakdowns in space and defending strongholds, about post-apocalyptic battles, chambers full of traps, using complicated devices, about zombies, traders... These are not in any way trivial riddles solvable in a mere five minutes, a simple matter of spotting the solution.

No way, these are difficult, complicated, brain teasing mini-games, full of tricky rules that you'll labor to solve, sometimes even for a good few hours.

My own puzzles, in fact, taught me, once and for all, a basic truth: **Players are more clever than me.**

'You are a squad leader fighting against the machines. You're in the trenches with your men. You have 21 seconds to disable the machines' group command center. A few soldiers, some equipment, the clock ticking, and a dozen machines in front of you: snipers, butchers, bombs. You have 21 seconds, go.' I had calculated it to the very second.

The replies come: 'Well, it goes as follows. First of all... ' - and there's a description of several sly moves, ending with: ' ... 14th second: detonate command center. Done. 14 seconds. The remaining 7 seconds we spend on cheering.'

There you have it. I spent an entire day on the design of this puzzle, I checked all the possibilities, corrected a lot, made it more difficult, streamlined... and this guy tells me, 'done in 14 seconds.'

In the next one I increase the difficulty level, and when I'm finally confident it is OK, it's published. The responses come in, and you guessed it, once again, they are better than I had thought possible. Once again, I underestimated the players' wits.

This was a while back, in the days when Portal was primarily a publisher of role-playing games and gaming magazines and I was preparing puzzles for our old magazine. It was a very important lesson I needed to learn before I started designing board games. I learned then that players are often more clever than the author. I started to respect the recipient, to respect the player.

As it happens, my board games that have been published up to now are in large part dynamic puzzles. Supposedly, every game is a kind of puzzle, but *Neuroshima Hex*, *Witchcraft* and *Theseus* are quite literally puzzles. Puzzles, so to speak, how I would conceive them - my style.

Each moment in *Neuroshima Hex*, *Theseus* or *Witchcraft* is a puzzle arranged on the board. You have a specific configuration of pawns in deadlock with one another, you have several locations with their unique characteristics, and – in your hand - a few possibilities of bringing some change to this frozen moment with different potentials. Each turn you solve a puzzle – you move, switch, add, turn, activate and there it is, this temporary puzzle solved, and then your opponent gets to solve his puzzle.

Puzzles - remember what I just wrote about puzzles and their recipients? I design a game, and even though I work on everything for months - polishing, testing, correcting, ascertaining the playability, boosting the balance, and Ignacy and I are working on it non-stop, - even though everything is tested by experienced playtesters, I still know that, in the end, it will end up in the hands of players who are much more cunning than any of us. Players, who after a couple months of playing, will be able to give me a hard time playing my own game.

One player might have a mathematical mind with a firm grasp on statistics, another may be a *Chess* or *Go* master, someone else may be very perceptive and sharp witted, never letting himself be taken by surprise, another will have a remarkable visual imagination, recreating without the slightest effort all the potential possibilities several turns ahead in his mind, whilst there will also be a brilliant strategist who sees through the game, knowing what is most important at any given moment. Finally, like some Neo from the Matrix, there will be a player who perceives the game as a great array of prime factors, and for him all the decisions and strategies will seem to be totally obvious.

I am aware that I am giving my game to such types of players to be devoured. This is not sending the game spiraling towards the abyss, but more often than not a positive situation. It's a bit like the reversal of apparent roles. I don't feel like a boss who sets his employees a task, but rather like a worker who offers up his work to the bosses. It teaches one humility and allows a slightly different perspective on the game - already while designing. Of course, it would have been the opposite were I designing games for kids. I would have assumed then that young players might have problems grasping possible tactics and thus, simplification would have been advisable.

But I don't make games for kids.

I create dynamic puzzles. And I know that the players are extremely cunning. That is why I respect the players' intelligence and I DON'T GIVE ready-made recipes for strategies and tactics in my games. I absolutely do not want to spoil the best part of the game for them, which is breaking it, creating monstrous combos, loops and totally uncontrollable 'abuses' of opportunities provided by the game elements.

I don't know about you, but for me this is the most enjoyable part of exploring any game. I've read the manual, and I am playing for the first time. It's a bit like crawling. I move, oh, I've even shot, oh, I've managed to move something. I slowly begin to get what this is about. Rules indeed seem trivial, but their usage itself has really a lot of subsequent layers.

I play a second time, a third, now moving freely and everything works. But this is only the tip of the iceberg. As there, underneath, hides a whole mountain of tactical possibilities of which I have no clue at this stage.

I play a hundredth time. I know the game quite well. But here I look at the situation on the board and, all of a sudden, I see a new possibility. I've discovered the meaning of yet another tactic that wasn't visible to me before.

I could cut the rules. Trim away card capabilities, board and unit powers. No one would notice the difference for the first dozen or so games. Everything would be more controlled, I would know exactly what those cunning players could come up with, what the possible configurations and situations were that could be boosted to perfection. This would be an easily describable number of possibilities that you simply have to use during the game. And be done. Check.

I might even describe them. Write a tactical tutorial at the back of the manual, putting forward in black and white, how the player should play step by step to play in the best possible way. What to do not to make mistakes in one's first games, make smooth use of all the game's possibilities from the start, not to do anything stupid, not to fall into a hopeless situation on the board, not to wander blindly.

I could force the players to play well using the rules, following the only proper tactics, perhaps with only a few degrees of variance, slightly worse, slightly better. Force them with 'closed' rules not to harm themselves, to play only in a more or less cost effective manner.

Oh no, I will not do that. I respect the intelligence of the players. My manual will not contain any kind of tutorial that breaks down tactical potential into prime factors.

What's more, I will absolutely not limit the possibilities in the game, nor the rules to a specific maximum. Cards, spaces on the board, tokens - all will have open rules, so a clever player, with substantial effort and crafty moves, will be able to put together such moves, with such possibilities too scary to contemplate. By launching the machine created on the board he will be able to utterly destroy his opponent in a hundred different ways. After all, these are dynamic puzzles, tactical 'Incredible Machines', and that is what this whole game is about! Every time you create a different machine, and from time to time you manage to create a real monster. You will have the feeling you've just broken the game, that what you've created should not have been possible. After all, it's a monster! And every time it will be a different kind of monster.

You know it from *Neuroshima Hex*. You will find it in *Theseus*. A lot of surprising intricacies await you there, you just have to master the game. I hope that this very discovery of more and more possibilities and always new layers of tactics will become the most enjoyable part of the game. So that, when you put together another combo creating 'unexpected' results, like with some Minecraft blocks, you will appreciate that they have not been announced in the rulebook or by the author as possibilities. You will have created something new.

For my own needs, I call it 'visible tactics' and 'hidden tactics'. Visible tactics are crystal-clear right after reading (and understanding) the manual. We know how to hit the enemy, how to move, how to place tiles, more or less what we have to do in order to win and how to do it. And we can play this way. Somebody wins, somebody loses, everything works. Only, that's not the point. Underneath the obvious moves there are a lot more layers of tactics hidden, a lot more less obvious moves and seemingly absolutely absurd ones, contradicting the first impression.

I once played a space strategy game on my PC, called The Outforce. Ah, good memories. The whole cosmic struggle in The Outforce relied on two simultaneous actions: expanding the base, powerful stationary defense systems on the one hand and expanding the fleet to carry out an assault on the enemy base on the other. The game was quite fun until I finally discovered it was possible to negate this game's seemingly only correct strategy. I discovered one could build a powerful missile defense wall around the base, then hook up tugs to it, accelerate them and let loose, so that, drifting through space, these powerful defensive and 'stationary' constructs could finally fall into the enemy base shooting missiles left and right. Then I truly fell in love with the game.

I had broken the game, I had created something unforeseen by the authors. I loved it. The game had hidden tactics. You could create something completely unexpected with the blocks provided by the designers. My satisfaction was huge.

The Outforce is an old game. Nowadays, computer games are more polished, tailored to the needs of today's customer. More and more often they will not let us wander and try, increasingly attempting to lead us by the hand. When we get lost for a moment in Dead Space (a modern video game), we simply press TAB and the path our hero should follow is highlighted in front of us. Pretty convenient, huh?

I don't think so. I feel sorry for those who like such assistance.

Dead Space is a great game, the battles here also resemble puzzles, but... these paths laid out in front of us... After all, we don't play games to pay homage to mental laziness, do we? The game itself can be a puzzle, not just a particular game move, but the entire game along with its hidden tactics. Discovering combos on your own, reaching dead ends, finding good and bad strategies, the side effects of moves, additional advantages of playing in a particular way – this is the flavor.

In *Neuroshima Hex*, the visible tactics are very simple. Place tiles so that as many as possible are aiming at the enemy headquarters. Start the battle only if you gain more than you lose. Protect your HQ from attacks.

Only with time you learn new blocks of hidden tactics. You notice that it is sometimes helpful to place a tile only to block a field your opponent could otherwise occupy. After many games you notice that it is not worthwhile starting the battle when you are in the lead and a situation is dangerous. That sometimes you have to sacrifice your good tile, not take advantage of its abilities at all, just to freeze the situation on the board for a bit longer. That sometimes you have to sacrifice a tile with no chance of survival in a given location - only to book yourself a place for the time after the battle to place another unit there. That sometimes you just have to quickly dump tiles from your hand and finish the game, not giving the opponent a chance to regain the lead.

You play better and better, being more and more aware of the game, understanding and using possible tactics, playing not as straightforward and direct as in the beginning, with catches and tricks at tournament level showing up.

In *Theseus*, the visible tactics are also simple. You just have to move the units to install and trigger cards and avoid the enemy's traps. Upgrade your units. Assume a good position. Trigger the onslaught. After all, that's the reason why you have all of this in your faction.

Scientists are to install cameras and gather recordings, examine intruders in their laboratories, hide and creep through secret passages to avoid the most dangerous places, use the medbay if necessary, install and activate defense systems, control the base with its blueprints and remote control. Aliens have to grow to their adult form as quickly as possible to be able to harm anyone at all, establish their nest, reproduce, seal the passages, move through ventilation systems and, in the end, kidnap or attack their opponents from hiding. Marines mainly have to install their battle stations, lay out mines, clear the premises with fire, secure their fortifications and lead the opponents straight into an ambush. The Greys are a bit more complicated, but everything is still clear and simple on this elementary level.

With time, however, you gradually discover further layers. You find that actions are best installed in tech bay, which sometimes allows you to use them even a few times during a turn. Then you discover this is not always for the best. All the things that help us in a regular fight should be gathered in the corridors, to allow them to always work immediately with the assault. You discover that duplicates are best placed in sectors with the greatest number of potential connections, that arrangements you have high hopes for should preferably be installed in sectors safe from the enemy's actions - like your own base.

After many games you'll discover that sometimes you need to place a card in a specific field only to book it for another card in the future, or to block it so that your opponent cannot create a deadly machine there. Or that it is worth taking the card only to get the bonus that may save you later from oppression. That sometimes you just have to speed up the game and, getting rid of the cards as quickly as possible, go straight to the final sequence. And that sometimes you have to even give up placing the card you would like to see on the board, only to prolong the game, should you need more time. The better you know the game, the more less obvious moves you begin to make.

Sometimes you'll move your units in order to activate a card, other times to develop your base or to install cards, to block the enemy, to prepare for greater movement opportunities in the following round, or to gather your forces for incoming assaults activated by card actions.

You won't have to spend much longer thinking about each round, you'll simply see a lot more. More and more things on the board will become obvious to you, and more and more you'll develop your own playing style. Because everyone plays in a somewhat different manner.

Whether or not the player will go as far as that in the game, will become absorbed, firstly depends on the game itself. Will the game draw him in? Make him addicted? Keep him coming back to play again and again? Secondly, it depends on whether the player enjoys exploring the secrets of the game, not visible at first glance, not described in black and white in the manual. I assume this is the case. Of course, not everyone enjoys this, but I know that for those puzzle-loving players it will be the lion's share of delight taken from the game. They have a lot to discover here, as I respect the player's intelligence and don't give much away in the manual. A final reason to want to explore a game fully is whether or not the player has confidence in the author.

But that I will discuss on another occasion.

Geoff Engelstein

Geoff
Engelstein

GEOFF
ENGELSTEIN

GEOFF ENGELSTEIN

GEOFF ENGELSTEIN

Geoff
Engelstein

GEOFF
ENGELSTEIN

Ignacy about Geoff:

It is hard to believe, but I remember the very first time I heard Geoff Engelstein's voice. I remember exactly when it was and where it was. I remember my excitement and I remember me going into our offices and talking about things I had just learned while driving my car and listening to The Dice Tower.

From that day onwards, the GameTek segment in The Dice Tower podcast became my favorite part of the show. Listening to Geoff is like going to your favorite lesson with your favorite teacher. He teaches about games (yay!) and does it in a very interesting way with lots of examples. He does amazing stuff. He knows about the construction of games, he knows the theory, he knows all that stuff behind the scenes that we gamers do not see when just playing a game and having fun. He is super educated.

I met Geoff for the first time at Gen Con 2013. He invited me to the Designers Panel organized by The Dice Tower. I was sitting next to him and during the entire panel discussion I had this very awkward feeling – each time Geoff began to talk, it felt like someone had just put headphones into my ears and I was once again listening to The Dice Tower. It was quite fun. Geoff is a super nice person, a great designer and... has an incredibly smart daughter – we played *Robinson Crusoe* the next day and I have to say, if not for Sydney and her ideas, everyone would have died miserably. She is amazing.

Geoff designed *The Ares Project*, a great RTS style game and two space opera style games - *Space Cadets* and *Space Cadets: Dice Duel*. Both of these space games have had a huge impact on our hobby, both got great reviews and both got nominations for the GoldenGeek Award Innovation category.

Knowing Geoff, I have to say - I am not surprised. I would be surprised, though, if his next game doesn't do the same.

Follow him on twitter: @gengelstein
You can listen to his podcast at http://ludology.libsyn.com/

BETWEEN DESPAIR AND HOPE

by Geoff Engelstein

Ignacy is waving a card in my face.

'This,' he says gravely, 'is the last good thing that is going to happen to you.'

It's Gencon 2013 and he is teaching me *Robinson Crusoe*. The card in question is 'Food Crates,' where much-needed provisions float off-shore. You just need to use some of your precious time to swim out and get them.

You're reading this, so I assume you've played, or at least are familiar with *Robinson Crusoe*. But just in case you're not, *Crusoe* is a series of scenarios that all have you and the other players washed ashore some terrible island, with something you need to accomplish to win. In the first scenario it seems fairly straightforward. You know a ship is going to be sailing by the island at a certain time. You need to build a big enough bonfire in order to attract their attention.

So all you need to do is collect enough wood. And not die in the meantime.

Unfortunately, there are many ways to die. Starvation. Depression. Goat attack. Falling off the roof of your hut while trying to repair it.

Of course, if you spend all of your time staying alive you won't get the wood for the fire. So you have to stay just alive enough in order to hang on until rescue.

Most games put the players in a heroic, larger than life role. Most games try to have epic scope, with the players cast in the leading roles. Save the kingdom. Liberate the galaxy. That kind of thing.

But not *Robinson Crusoe*. Its victories are small victories. Enough food in your belly. A patchwork roof to see you through the night. And you play a Cook or Carpenter, not a Wizard or Warrior.

So why is it popular? Why do people love it so? What's the attraction in sliding inexorably towards a mundane death?

How can a game be so thoroughly cruel to its players, but keep drawing them back for more?

First, while there is an unrelenting stream of bad things happening to your poor group of castaways, hope is right there in front of you. Hope in the form of simple inventions to make your life a little more bearable. Fire. Snares. A spear. A shovel.

You know what all the items are. There's no 'quad turbo RX32 ion blasters' to be built. There's a spear, or a hole in the ground to keep food. You know what these things are and what they can do. You know deep down why you want all these incredibly primitive but incredibly necessary inventions spread out across the table.

The game suspends you between despair and hope.

The whole array of what you could have and what would make things so much better is tantalizingly displayed right in front of you. They are not just in a deck of cards that you draw from hoping to get what might help. They are all just out there, in hand's reach, both beckoning and taunting you.

Taunting because you know that you'll probably hurt yourself trying to build them, as you have a dreaded 'adventure'. These adventures are not like *You find a hidden cave and discover a temple built by an ancient civilization.* These adventures are *Accident. Through inattention you cut your leg with a tool. It may get worse.*

So why is this fun? Isn't it much more interesting to find that ancient civilization than to get gangrene?

Why? Because it puts me right into the action. Me as in ME. Not me as Intergalactic Starship Captain, but me as Geoff Engelstein. Because although I know how to program a computer, if I were stranded on a desert island I am pretty sure I would give myself gangrene trying to make a shovel.

Which brings me to my second point. All the damage in *Robinson Crusoe* is self-inflicted. At least, it is cleverly designed to seem self--inflicted.

If I want to build that shovel I have two choices. I can put both of my action markers on the build action and build it with no risk at all. Or I can try to do two things this turn, rushing both, and chancing a problem. So when I get gangrene it's not the game (or more properly, Ignacy) that's causing a problem. I've brought this on myself.

Certainly a situation I've caused in the real world.

And just in case you missed the fact that you chose to rush through shovel construction, the adventure card is there to remind you:

Accident. Through inattention you cut your leg with a tool. It may get worse.

This is all your fault, klutz!

So we turn on ourselves. We don't blame the game for hitting us with random horribleness. We blame ourselves. If only... If only I had spent more time on the shovel. If only I hadn't chosen to hunt. If only I had reinforced the roof.

The genius of *Robinson Crusoe* is that it gives you two terrible options and then gets you to blame yourself when the choice you pick turns out to be, well, terrible.

But there's one more element that elevates Robinson Crusoe from horrible to memorable. The design builds up tremendous tension.

As Alfred Hitchcock said of suspense: 'There's two people having breakfast and there's a bomb under the table. If it explodes, that's a surprise. But if it doesn't...'

In too many games the bomb goes off right away. You turn over a card and something bad happens.

But not *Robinson Crusoe*. Let's go back to that Accident card, where you cut your leg with a tool. Remember the end of the flavor text?

It may get worse.

Yup. When you draw that card it does nothing. The person that drew it just puts a marker on the leg of their character. There's no immediate effect on the game at all. Carry on as usual.

But you also shuffle the card into the event deck. And if it gets drawn again, then you do actually get gangrene. And bad things happen.

Of course you don't know if it will get drawn. It may never get drawn. You may win before then. Or die. And there's a way to mitigate it. You can use one of your precious actions to get the healing herbs. Instead of, you know, eating, or getting that wood you need to win.

So the bomb just sits under the table ticking away.

And of course, when it explodes it'll be your fault. You didn't have to rush building the shovel. And once you cut yourself you could have gotten the medicine. But you didn't. Shame on you.

Cliffhangers have been tried in games before. *Fortune and Glory* puts your character in a tough spot and then ends your turn. So you have to wait until you get to go again before seeing if you survived driving your motorcycle off of the cliff or not. But you can't do anything about it in the meantime. And you know it will be on your very next turn. So it's just a waiting game.

Compare that with not knowing how many turns you have until the gangrene hits, and trying to figure out if you want to get that medicine or not. That's a much more interesting situation, and one much more rife with tension and angst.

And so we keep coming back to play *Robinson Crusoe* again and again. To try not to make so many mistakes. To try to master our own impulsiveness.

I've only had the pleasure of meeting Ignacy a few times. And he has always struck me as a very nice guy.

But for such a nice guy, he seems to revel in misfortune.

He is clear with designers that if he publishes your game you'd better not be too attached to it. He plans on ripping it to pieces and rebuilding it better than it was. His focus on testing and tweaking over and over again almost drove Michał Oracz to pick up *Theseus* and go home. And as a player, if you aren't focused during one of his games, well, you won't be happy with the result.

I take that back. Ignacy doesn't revel in misfortune. He is hyper--focused on making games the best they can be, even at the expense of the feelings of both designers and players.

But it's worth it in the end. Because – let's face it – I need to learn how to make a shovel without getting gangrene.

Bruno
Cathala

Bruno Cathala

BRUNO
CATHALA

BRUNO CATHALA

Bruno
Cathala

BRUNO CATHALA

BRUNO
CATHALA

Ignacy about Bruno:

I met Bruno for the first time at Essen 2006. I got his autograph and ran off. I met him again at Essen 2007, and Essen 2008 and in all the years after. He knew who I was. I knew who he was. We passed each other, saying 'Hi' for years. I respected his work and believed that Bruno had no reason to talk to a kid like me. So I didn't impose.

In 2013 Merry and I were invited to Bruno Faidutti's Gathering of Friends. Of course I ran into Bruno Cathala there, I said 'Hi,' and things would have continued like they always had, but...

It was Saturday morning. Merry and I walked into the dining room. There were many free tables and only one person in the whole room. Bruno. So, as you might expect, I said 'Hi,' made myself some tea and moved towards a free table. Merry – who is my dearest precious – pinched me very painfully and whispered: 'You must be kidding!' She took her coffee and went directly to Bruno's table.

And that is how everything changed.

Bruno is the funniest designer I have ever met. And I have to say, most designers are pretty funny. But he is just brilliant. He tells anecdotes one after another, great little jokes with precisely constructed punch lines and funny comments while discussing any topic. That weekend in France we played his prototype (a game that will be published by Days of Wonder in 2014, of which the title has not yet been announced at the time of writing this) and it was a blast. An amazing game. Or rather *another* amazing game, because Bruno's bio is filled with great designs like *Shadows over Camelot, Mr. Jack* and *Cyclades.* My personal pick? *Boomtown.* One of the most underestimated games on this planet. Gamers, you need to check it out. And his new game from Days of Wonder too, of course.

And all of his other games!

 Follow him on twitter: @BDMontagnes
Subscribe to: http://bruno-des-montagnes.over-blog.com/

THE FIRST TIME

by Bruno Cathala

We all know that, regardless of the topic, 'the first time' will always remain something special, something unforgettable. Therefore, I've chosen to share with you some of my first times.

My first modern game experience
I discovered modern games quite late. I was 18 years old when I purchased *Fief*, just because it was recommended by a French magazine specialized in games (Jeux & Stratégie, which closed its doors in 1989). This game had just won the 'Pion d'or' award, run by Jeux & Stratégie, for which designers sent in games, with the winner getting published.

The first thing I noticed about the game was its rules – they immediately put a big smile on my face. The turn sequence included something I had had no experience with so far: a secret negotiation phase. It seemed really exciting. And what was most interesting about this was that the rules clearly stated that doing what you promised was not mandatory. Wow, this was definitely a game for me!

With my friends, we played Fief a lot. Each time there was a lot of tension, including spectacular backstabs, and sometimes grudges were borne for weeks... Each time there would be someone swearing they would never play such a game again... and each time they would return to the table shortly after. This incredible gaming experience led me to two conclusions:

Yes, there was life after *Monopoly.*

One day I would create my own game.

My first game design experience
After this first revelation, even though I wanted to create my own game one day, things didn't quite work out that way, for various reasons. First of all, it is impossible to create an interesting game if you have not experienced for yourself the many different types of games available nowadays. For years, therefore, I was just a player. I read all I could find concerning games (in magazines and on internet sites), and I got the chance to try out the many different styles of game play in modern games.

Secondly, I had no time to really think about game creation. I was working in Research & Development at Tungsten Alloys (don't worry, it's not contagious), I was deeply involved in my local rugby team, and if you add two small children to the mix, you will understand that 24 hours a day is still not enough.

In 1999 things changed. I broke my knee, and had to stop rugby, and I got divorced. Then, one November weekend, for the first time in years, I was home alone. No rugby, no wife, no children, no friends. It was a strange and rather unpleasant feeling. It seemed I had to choose fast between suicide or doing something to bring some excitement back into my life. As you might already have understood, I chose the second option.

I headed into town to buy a clipart library. After installing it on my computer I began to think... First I would need to consider components... why not make a card game? This was my first try at this, and cards are easy to create. Next, the story... well... Why not go with Western. The far west seemed perfect to me. It's wild, cruel, with a lot of colorful characters. You don't have to be realistic, you can include humor, and it reminded me of a lot of evenings with my dad watching classic Westerns on TV.

At that point, I had no idea what to do concerning game mechanisms. I simply began to select pictures which could fit with my Western idea.

The far west meant Ranch. Ranch meant cows. So I needed images of a cow, but... in my clipart library there were hundreds of cows... I selected three of them, thinking I would choose one of them later. Now I had to feed the cows. I looked for western landscapes, and selected three of those too. Next up were the cowboys to herd the cows – three of those were soon found as well.

Now I had three cows, a fat one, a normal one and a very slim one. I had three landscapes, one grassy, one standard, and one barren. Finally, I had three cowboys: an experienced hand, a regular, and a rookie. What I did not expect was that looking at this seemingly random choice, all the mechanisms needed for this game fell into place:

Depending on the quality of the grass, a land could receive from 1 to 3 Cow cards.

Depending of the quality of the cows, the price would vary.

Depending on how long they would stay in their fields, their quality would increase.

Depending on the quality of the cowboys, it would be easier or more difficult not to waste cows.

Now all I needed was to add some special cards to include interaction and fun. This led me to create some cards like 'Indian raid,' 'Railway station,' 'Panic,' and 'Sheriff.' At the end of the weekend, the first prototype of *Sans Foi Ni Loi* (*Lawless*) was finished. 110 cards, just printed and cut, were waiting for a first testing session.

Three days later, my friends came to visit and we played our first game. We were surprised to find that the game worked really well without any major issues from the beginning to the end. The game length was alright, we had a lot of fun, and everybody immediately wanted to play a second game, even though some of the cards weren't well balanced at this point.

My first contact with a publisher

After this first, very positive test session, I spent December 1999 improving my prototype. In early January 2000, this work seemed to me to be finished. I certainly didn't think I had designed the best game in the world, but I was convinced that I would be able to find worse games already published. So now it was time to contact publishers in order to find out if my feeling was right or if I should just give up wanting to become a game designer.

I live in the French Alps, far from Paris and all the French game companies. At this time, furthermore, I had absolutely no contacts in the gaming industry. I figured that the well-known publishers were big companies, and that if I wrote them, chances were that my mail would simply not reach the right people. Therefore, I decided to focus on smaller companies.

Some months earlier I had noticed the creation of a new game company, which had just published two games at the same time, *Lyonesse*, a really nice Role Playing Game based on Jack Vance's stories, and *Dirty Christmas*, a small card game, with nice and humoristic artwork. It was immediately clear that my game would fit nicely in the same line as this card game. The games had the same number of cards (110), were fast and fun to play, and contained humor.

The name of the company was 'Men in Cheese... this name made me think that they were probably from Switzerland. On the internet, I did some research and found a phone number and an address in Geneva - indeed Switzerland, and only 25 km from home! I grabbed my phone and gave them a call.

Me: Hello! Men in Cheese?

Them: Yes?

Me: I've seen your two new games and just noticed that you were based very close to where I live. I'm a game designer and I would like to know if you are looking for new games.

Them: Yes, of course... well.. what are you doing tomorrow evening? If you have some prototypes you could show us, we would be happy to test them!

Me: Alright, I'd love to! See you tomorrow...

Incredible, I got a meeting! The next day I went to Geneva to meet them. My first surprise, at the address, was that the name of the publisher, 'Men in Cheese was only a mail address. The address actually belonged to an advertising company. They explained to me that this advertising company was their real job, and that game publishing was just their passion, and that they were working on games as a hobby.

The second surprise I got was that the team was composed of just two guys and no one else... The evening was very pleasant. We played my game three times and we all had great fun. At the end of the evening they stepped out for 10 minutes to discuss, and then returned to tell me what they had decided.

'We like your game a lot, and we have decided to publish it. The only issue is that to produce it, we need money. And we have just launched two games. Therefore, we will need to wait some months to earn back some money from the sale of these two games, and as soon as that has been accomplished, we can produce yours. If you agree, during this waiting period you could come with us to some Role Playing Game conventions. That way you will be able to demonstrate your prototype to create some buzz and do some fine tuning in the process. Does that sound alright to you?'

It definitely sounded alright to me! I had been in the game design business for just a month, and already someone was offering to publish my game... That evening, when I got back home, I felt like the king of the world, and I wondered whether I was dreaming...

Now the most frustrating part of being a game designer started: waiting! For more than a year, I just waited... I joined them at two RPG conventions. An interesting experience, because at those kind of conventions, people come for RPGs, not for board or card games. Each time, I had some difficulty convincing people to come and play the first game. But then, once they were playing, the great atmosphere created by the prototype was contagious enough to attract new players, and my table was never empty.

During all this time, I shared all my ideas with Men in Cheese, and gave them all the latest prototype files (the updated rules and everything else that is needed to print prototypes and work with an illustrator). I stayed in touch with them via mail or phone on average about once a week for an entire year.

And then suddenly, there was no more news. Something really strange and disturbing happened. I called the two guys on their personal and work phone numbers, emailed them at their personal and work email addresses, and all gave the same answer. 'This phone number (or mail address) doesn't exist anymore.'

I jumped into my car and drove to Geneva... the advertising company had closed. Ouch!

I had no actual contract for my game. And they had all my files. And considering that it's virtually impossible to protect game ideas, I began to fear they could produce my game at a different company without me. My dream seemed to have turned into a nightmare.

My first contact with an experienced game designer

You can imagine how this situation stressed me. No news... and this fear that I would be cheated out of my own game .. this led to a feeling of desperation. I had nothing more to lose, so why not try something crazy?

As explained previously, before creating my own game I had tried to learn everything there was to know about games from magazines and internet websites. One of these sources was Bruno Faidutti's website (and his famous ideal game library). As a gamer, I liked his game design (in particular *Knightmare Chess*, *Citadels* and *Mystery of the Abbey*). I also liked the way he wrote about games on his website. And there, in his introduction, he wrote: 'For 10 years now I have been designing games, alone or in collaboration.'

Well, I thought, why not write him and propose a collaboration?

I sent him a mail explaining shortly (in less than 10 lines) the history of my game. I then proposed that he would become co-designer of my game if he thought he could find a publisher. Frankly speaking, I never thought he would answer me.

Two hours later, I received a mail from him. I will always remember how concise it was:

'Hello,

Send me your prototype.

I see 3 solutions:

I don't like it and I'll send it back to you.

I like it and I will help you finish it: if we find a publisher, we co--sign it.

I like it but there is really nothing to do: if I find a publisher for you, I would just like you to give me 10 copies of the game for the prize table of my game event that I organize each year.'

Once more it was hard to believe that someone I didn't know personally would offer to help me this way...

So, I sent my prototype. Two weeks later I received a new mail from Bruno (the real one... in the game industry I'm just the other Bruno): 'We played your game and liked it a lot. There is nothing more to do. I will do my best to convince Jeux Descartes to publish it.' And he did! Bruno, once more, I have to tell you I will never forget the incredible opportunity you gave me... Thanks!

My first real contract

Some months later, as promised by Bruno, Jeux Descartes contacted me regarding the contract. They invited me to join them in Lyon, in a game shop belonging to the company. They were organizing a small meeting there, with local designers, to see if some prototypes would fit their product line. They explained to me that it would be a good opportunity to meet me face to face and to sign the contract.

So I headed for Lyon in my car - two hours of driving.

You have to understand that for me, being late to a meeting is impossible. This meant that I was there 15 minutes in advance. The Head of Publishing was already there. He wanted to play my *Sans Foi Ni Loi* with me. However, as the game was not designed for two players, we had to wait for the other people to arrive.

I asked him if he would be interested in trying another prototype. A 2-player game. You see, during the long year I had to wait for Men in Cheese to publish my game, I had spent some hours designing a small 2-player game, a pirate game that was called *No Mercy* at the time. He answered that he would be happy to try it out, because he was looking to create a specific 2-player game line, but had nothing interesting to start with.

So we played a first game of *No Mercy*. And I won. An overwhelming defeat for him... He looked at me, smiling, and said: 'Well, it's not really smart of you to humiliate someone who might publish you.' I answered: 'Well, I think that a conscientious publisher, from this first experience, would understand that this small game is not based on luck, but on strategy. And that he would like to test the learning curve.' He said: 'Alright, let's play again immediately.'

Our second game had the same result. I won. His score was better but still far from mine. And he said: 'Let's play another game.' At this point, all the other people we were waiting for had already arrived.

They were standing by, spectators to our amicable confrontation. The third game I won as well. This time, however, the final score was closer. He said nothing more, and the real meeting began. All the other designers showed their prototypes. We also played *Sans Foi Ni Loi*.

At the end of the afternoon, I stayed alone with the Head of Publications to sign the contract for *Sans Foi Ni Loi*. Before leaving, I asked him:

Me: 'And my small 2-player game? Do you think you would be interested?'

Him: 'Yes, definitely. It's exactly what I'm looking for. But to launch a 2-player game line, I need at least three games. Here, I have only one.'

He smiled and added: 'Now you know what you have to do!'

Me: 'Are you serious? If I come to you with two other 2-player games, you'll publish all of them?'

Him: 'As long as they are of the same quality as this one, yes!'

Once more, I found myself in an incredible situation... proving that I'm definitely a lucky guy!

I went back home, wondering if I would be able to create these new games. Three months later, I had them. And Jeux Descartes indeed chose to publish them. In the end they decided to publish these 2-player games before *Sans Foi Ni Loi*. And this is the reason why, appearing out of nowhere, my first three games were published at the same time at the Essen fair in 2002. The names of these games?

Guerre & Bêêêh (*War & Sheep*)

Tony & Tino

Drake and Drake (previously known as *No Mercy*)

Sans Foi Ni Loi (*Lawless*) was released some months later in April 2003.

Rustan Håkansson

Rustan Håkansson

RUSTAN
HÅKANSSON

RUSTAN HÅKANSSON

RUSTAN HÅKANSSON

Rustan
Håkansson

RUSTAN
HÅKANSSON

Ignacy about Rustan:

I met Rustan at Essen 2007. A long time ago. He visited our booth, bought *Neuroshima Hex* and soon after became one of the most active and creative fans worldwide. We stayed in touch for years. We met every year in Essen and had a talk about *Neuroshima Hex*, his new fan armies and games in general.

In 2011 I asked Rustan if he would be interested in Portal Games publishing one of his fan armies for *Neuroshima Hex* as an official army. He agreed. We accepted *The Dancer* for publication, and that is how we began a new chapter for the *Neuroshima Hex* line. Fan armies and the best of fan created content now have the chance to be a part of the official line. By publishing Rustan's *The Dancer* we sent a very clear message to our fans. We look forward to seeing your content. So far it has worked out very well.

The Dancer was released in 2012 and got amazing reviews. A year after that release Rustan had another release, this time much bigger – his *Nations* was one of the biggest hits of Essen 2013. Like every year he visited our booth at Essen, got our new releases, had a chat with us and then went back to take care of his own game, *Nations*.

Without a doubt we will meet again next year at Essen, and the year after that, to discuss *Neuroshima Hex* and other games. And without a doubt, Rustan will have a few more great games released in the following years. With his first designs, among which a number of different fan armies for *Neuroshima Hex*, he has proven to be a very creative person. I am eager to see what is next from his designer's desk!

 Follow him on twitter: @rustan_h

CONCEPTS TO PROTOTYPES

by Rustan Håkansson

I like the initial concept stage of game creation best. Anything can be imagined and changes are so easy when you can switch out half the game in a thought. A game idea can start from anything and focus on either theme or mechanic. Many months can go by without a single idea, but when I am in the right mood I often have many in a day. This correlates so strongly with stress levels at my day job that I use it to find out if I need to reduce the pace at work.

The most intense concept phase I have been in was probably a stretch of 4 days when I made lots and lots of concepts for armies and scenarios for *Neuroshima Hex*, one of them being *The Dancer* army that was published 2012. I posted *The Dancer* and some of the others on BGG, and several of those now have prototype tiles and work fairly well. Thank you Michałlus, Midaga and everyone else who has helped! One of the armies that I was pleased with is the Super Mutant Killer Bunnies (inspired by the killer rabbit in Monty Python's Quest for the Holy Grail). I thought mutated monster rabbits would be perfect for a fun Easter downloadable file. The tiles were super-pink and that together with the name 'Bunnies' made Ignacy and others who know the Neuroshima story well just shake their heads.

When an idea has started to settle in my mind I write it down. This is a really important step as it forces all the loose ends to show how they can be connected. This is also when I decide to either file away the concept for later or to start on a prototype. Some concepts change drastically when writing them down! Very few are so interesting that I start making a prototype. Of those maybe half survive initial mechanics / solo tests and get played with an opponent. After a couple of games I need to decide if I want to develop it further.

Prototyping is another phase I enjoy. I like physically creating things: cutting, gluing and the feeling of having made something new. As a kid I constructed lots of buildings for model railroads and enjoyed making paper cutouts. During my university years my gaming focus was on miniature games: playing, painting and building terrain. My wife Nina (co-designer of *Nations*) and I arranged a *Confrontation* tournament for 40 players using only our own terrain. Now making prototypes fills this desire to create.

Making the prototype look good is important to me. It does not need to have great art or graphics, but it needs to be clean and clear. Components need to make sense from the start. I have lots of generic cubes and borrow parts from other games as needed. Most custom components are cards, chits and boards. The free computer program Nandeck is great for this; without it, *Nations* would be only half-way finished by now. At one point we had close to 500 cards and wanted to test a big restructuring of costs and production. Thanks to Nandeck it was fairly quick to do that.

A laminator is really important for creating cards that need to be shuffled. I use sleeves sometimes but it does not give the same feeling, and does not work with smaller tiles. When I bought the laminator I was very picky and returned 4 different models before I found one that did not create bubbles. It was some years ago though, so quality might have improved now.

I like to have printed backs for tiles and cards. They do not need to be fancy, but I'd much rather spend the extra time needed to set up basic backs than to improve the fronts. It makes the whole prototype feel more like a real game. I dislike anonymous piles and constantly forgetting which one is which. I find it is easier to get playtesters to give useful feedback if they are not hindered by confusing components.

I scribble small changes on components after playtests, but normally run at most 2-3 test games in that state before I create a new prototype. We have a large box of saved prototype components from *Nations*, despite throwing away a lot of it.

Often during development I try to think about what is special about a game, what makes it stand out. If I cannot answer this I'll file it away. I've worked on some prototypes just because they felt good enough to be published games, but were not great for at least some players. I just grew bored while working on them, so I stopped. There is no reason to create a good enough game when so many great ones exist. After playtest sessions I always ask if the players enjoyed it and would play again. If not I tend to rework before testing further.

Another question I ask myself many times during development is what the core of the game is. This helps to identify what parts are candidates for removal. Thinking through how the game would be without something, and testing that, is important. If the game is still fun and interesting it is almost always good to make it simpler and shorter. And adding something back later if needed is a lot easier than seeing that something should be removed.

The development of *Nations* was a bit different for me as there were four of us in the project, and an explicit reason we started it was to keep in touch. Changing something was not that easy and on many occasions took a lot of time. A common situation was that one wanted a change, two were against it, and the fourth was annoyed we got stuck on such a minor detail. And minor detail it could really be, like a single value change on a single card that caused endless email discussions, multiple phone discussions and many playtests to settle.

On the other hand it was also very good to be four on the project. Someone else could solve something when one got stuck. Different skills and preferences in games complemented each other and caused new ideas to form when we could not agree on either using normal thematic (Robert) nor euro (Rustan) mechanics for something (with Einar and Nina more balanced). The most important part was that we all helped to keep the project going for so many years.

My son is finally old enough to understand and enjoy games in which you play with real rules. Current favorites are *Zooloretto Mini* and *Castle Panic*. When he was smaller I mostly improvised games using both kids and adult games, but now that he can play I expect more of my prototypes in the near future to be kids games. However, at the moment my focus is on several projects for *Nations* that we hope will get published too!

Seiji
Kanai

Seiji Kanai

SEIJI
KANAI

SEIJI KANAI

SEIJI KANAI

Seiji
Kanai

SEIJI
KANAI

Ignacy about Seiji:

'What's this?' I asked when Piechu showed us *Love Letter* at Essen 2012.

'I don't know. I bought a different game and they gave me a discount on this. It was cheap,' he answered.

'I am not surprised,' I said, looking at the game. You know, it was just a few cards. 'Are you sure it isn't a promo or some such crap?' He didn't know. He threw the game into his luggage and we forgot about it. How could I have known that I was holding a revolution in my hands?!

William Attia changed our hobby with *Caylus* and its worker placement mechanism, Donald X. Vaccarino changed our hobby with *Dominion* and its deckbuilding mechanism, and Seiji Kanai changed it with *Love Letter* and its micro game format. Pure fun hidden in 16 cards. Brilliant. I can't express how much I respect Kanai, or how impressed I am by this game. Seeing all those micro games published these days, I am not the only one, right?

I do have *R.R.R.* and *Love Letter* in my collection and I am looking forward to playing Kanai's other games. This is a designer who did something extraordinary. *Love Letter* is a game that will be remembered 10, 15, even 20 years from now. It has started a new trend.

I have not had the chance to meet Seiji in person yet, but I am very proud that he agreed to contribute to this book. And I think you will not be surprised that his article is quite short. Micro style it is! :)

 Follow him on twitter: @KanaiSeiji

THE MOST IMPORTANT THING WHEN CREATING A GAME

by Seiji Kanai

What is it that you really need in order to create a game?

Is it the money required for printing it? Or an illustrator who can faithfully visualize your idea? Or is it just a bright mind, that fluently can manipulate various game systems?

Naturally, should you have all that, creating a game would probably be pretty smooth. But having only the above isn't enough. Or at least, that is how I see it.

For as long as I've been doing this, I've been meeting a lot of people, among whom people who want to create games or want to write novels. Like them, I was once there, coming up with epic back-stories, fantasy or science fiction, and characters that populated these back-stories.

Sadly, though, few of these people ever make anything interesting. And you won't find any of my stories in book stores either.

The reason for this is that their ideas never left their heads.

An idea, regardless of how brilliant and fantastic it may be, is worth nothing as long as it's just in someone's head. It's like a rough gem, buried in the ground. Until it's dug up and people can see it, it cannot be polished, and it cannot be valued. It's only when it has left the ground that it starts to reflect the light and can start to shine.

What I believe is the most important thing you need to do in order to create a game (or anything, for that matter), is to take the idea out of your head, and put it into some physical form that can be viewed and touched.

It's true that just a piece of thick carton with weird crayon lines on it, and hand-cut, hand-written cards, isn't something that will impress. And as long as the rules are just in your head and not on paper, you might have a hard time explaining them, and whoever you called up to test-play might just frown and grimace. But it's only when you manage to actually try playing, that the game creation process begins.

And when you play it again the following week or the following month, your game might make people smile instead.

Or as I read somewhere: 'Hard work doesn't always result in success. But successes have invariably started with hard work.'

Mike
Selinker

Mike Selinker

MIKE
SELINKER

MIKE SELINKER

MIKE SELINKER

Mike
Selinker

MIKE
SELINKER

Ignacy about Mike:

You probably all know this story - Michael Jordan led the Chicago Bulls to the NBA championship for three years in a row, being the best NBA player of his time. Then he retired from basketball to play baseball. With Jordan having retired, great young players like Hakeem Olajuwon and Shaquille O'Neal grabbed their chance to become legends of the NBA. They played amazing basketball and were the great stars of the league. Then suddenly, Jordan decided to come back. He led the Chicago Bulls to another three championships in a row in 1996, 1997, and 1998. He left no doubt as to who was the best basketball player on the planet.

For me, Mike Selinker is just like Michael Jordan.

Mike has been designing great games for ages. When I was a kid in high school I was playing RPGs that he was involved in. Then, when I stood at the beginning of my board game adventure and was trying to design something interesting, he was already winning Origins Awards for his great *Pirates of the Spanish Main*, *Axis & Allies: D-Day*, and *Betrayal at House on the Hill*. He was always there. A top notch designer.

Over the past few years some great new designers have been born; guys like Chvatil, Bauza and Vaccarino created great games and became authors known worldwide.

We players might have forgotten about Selinker.

But then suddenly, in 2013, Selinker decided to make a come back. He published *Pathfinder*. It was like a damn roller. The most discussed, most played, most hyped, most recommended game in the US in 2013. All of Gen Con just went crazy about this game. The reviewers. The geeks. In a few months it went straight into the Top 50 at BGG.

I am back, said Selinker, and showed everybody else their place. It was an epic comeback.

I have never met Mike in person, but I hope I will meet him some day. And I cannot wait to see his new game. I hope you can't wait either.

 Follow him on twitter: @mikeselinker
Subscribe to: http://www.lonesharkgames.com/

CURING THE PANDEMIC PROBLEM

by Mike Selinker

Matt Leacock's *Pandemic* is a fabulous game. If it's not on your list of the top 100 board games, you died in 2007. I can't really help you with that problem, except to suggest you get more brains in your diet.

Pandemic is a cooperative game in which the world is threatened by deadly diseases. You work as a team, each player having a role such as Researcher or Containment Specialist. The game tries to beat you into the ground, but if you strategize, you might be able to arrest the contagion and save the world. Might.

It is, as I said, a fabulous game. But it has a serious flaw, one it shares with *Forbidden Island* and *Flash Point* and other such cooperative games.

Pandemic, not surprisingly, falls prey to the Pandemic Problem.

The Pandemic Problem is a meta-problem. It's not a flaw of the rules or the intended gameplay, which in the case of *Pandemic* are stellar. It's a problem with the people playing it. To explain it, I have to go back to the origins of roleplaying games.

When *Dungeons & Dragons* first walked the earth in the 1970s, it described a player called the 'caller'. This wasn't a character class like fighter or cleric. It was an out-of-game role which complemented the 'mapper', whose job it was to draw the map of the dungeon. The caller's job was to survey what the mapper drew and make strategic decisions for the entire adventuring party. A caller might have said the following:

'The fighter charges the bugbear while the wizard peppers his goblin thugs with magic missiles. Meanwhile, the elf sneaks behind the bugbear and backstabs him.' Note that it's not clear from that statement which character the caller was playing. It's irrelevant.

He played *all of them*.

With one person making the calls, the game was an evenly balanced experience. The Dungeon Master played one side, and the caller—ably abetted by the rest of the party, as needed—played the other. All that remained was some rolling of dice.

As later editions of *D&D* came out, the role of the caller diminished, then vanished completely. The game designers realized that players wanted to make their own decisions, so designating one person to speak for everyone was counterproductive. The initiative system, which determined an order in which characters would act, rendered the caller obsolete, since the spotlight shined on each player in sequence.

Flash forward to the 1980s, when semi-cooperative board games appeared. The nearly identical games *Scotland Yard* and *The Fury of Dracula* each featured a bad-guy player (Mr. X and Dracula, respectively), and everyone else battled against him. This neatly paralleled the Dungeon Master/players dynamic of RPGs, and the Pandemic Problem was born, twenty years before *Pandemic*.

In a game of *The Fury of Dracula*, the hunters would plot against the Dracula player, and then, more often than not, one hunter would say something like this:

'Lord Godalming goes to Barcelona, then Dr. Seward goes to Clermont-Ferrand, and then Van Helsing goes to Zagreb.'

On its face, there's nothing wrong with this type of strategizing. Having a 'lead hunter' made everyone's job easier, since all players, including the Dracula player, would know what was coming. The problem came when the player saying that wasn't really interested in anyone else's opinion. It would come out like this.

'Okay, you go to Barcelona, and you go to Clermont-Ferrand. Then I'll go to Zagreb. That's what we're doing.'

Now, no one was holding a gun to these players' heads. Some of them might've wanted a charismatic commander. But some wanted to go home. Reduced to watching two players play, Dracula and the leader of the hunters, some players found something better to do with their time. I have seen it happen.

For me, the clear alternative was Chaosium's *Arkham Horror*. This was a fully cooperative game, where the goal was to shut the portal to a non-Euclidean dimension of implacable Lovecraftian horrors. *Arkham Horror* never fell victim to the Pandemic Problem, because the Doom Track made it nearly impossible to strategize. You were always under the presumption that the game was going to kill everyone, and if you somehow avoided being sucked up into the Dreamlands by Ithaqua on turn two, you'd have a chance to save the town of Arkham. Probably not, though.

While fun, this was less than ideal. Making sure the world ended before coordination could ensue was not the solution. I needed to try to solve the problem at its core.

My first attempt came in 2003, when I started working on *Betrayal at House on the Hill*. Funny story about that: It nearly never happened. In 1995, designer Bruce Glassco submitted his 'House on the Hill' prototype to Avalon Hill, which was in a world of hurt. The company was eventually consumed by Hasbro, and designers Mike Gray and Rob Daviau found Glassco's dusty submission among the wreckage. They tried in vain to launch it as a Hasbro product, but their marketing colleagues were having none of it.

'Let's see,' they said. 'A semi-cooperative RPG-lite game with cards, dice, tiles, plastic figures, punch-out tokens, and three rule books? Right. Where's the next *Elefun?*'

I assumed control of Avalon Hill's R&D in early 2003 while at Wizards of the Coast. Rob showed me the House on the Hill prototype, and I fell in love. I promised Rob that I would find a way to get this game out.

We had clear plans for three games: Larry Harris's and my reboot of *Axis & Allies*, a game for the 60th anniversary of D-Day, and my own *Risk Godstorm*, designed with Mike Donais and Rich Baker. None of those were originally Avalon Hill titles. We were charting new territory here with those first three releases, which were guaranteed hits. But the brand team demanded a fourth game.

'I have *Betrayal*!' I said. 'It's a semi-cooperative RPG-lite game with cards, dice, tiles, plastic figures, punch-out tokens, and three rulebooks!'

You can guess how that went. I got the same reaction that the Hasbro guys did: too many parts, too cooperative, too weird. So I sent the brand team on a quixotic quest to secure the rights to *Titan*, a board game by the noted recluse Dave Trampier. As I heard it, Tramp told them to get the hell off his lawn. With *Titan* now impossible, I was asked if I had something—anything—else.

'I have *Betrayal*!' I said.

'Fine, whatever,' they said, and we were off to the races. I put a genius development team on recasting Bruce's brilliant game, steeping it in a bizarre world of vampires and zombies.

Betrayal solved the caller problem by introducing a new complication: It was fully cooperative, right up until the point that it wasn't. *Betrayal* introduced a traitor mechanic, which worked like this: During the Exploration phase, all players enter the haunted house with no clear idea of what the problem in the house is. They'd pick up items like the Blood Dagger, and run into events like the Revolving Wall. Along the way, they'd amass a number of Omens—scary things that heightened the suspense—until someone rolled a haunt roll equal to or less than the number of Omens. Then the world changed.

Now, in the Haunt phase, a random player left the room to read a scenario page from the traitor book, and turned against the rest of the group. The others read a different page, and tried to figure out what to do. When the traitor came back in the room, filled with the power of werewolves or aliens or horrors from beyond the pale, the other players would do their best to stop the traitor from killing them all.

So why didn't *Betrayal* fall prey to the caller problem? Well, let's step back a bit. I mentioned that in the Exploration phase, everybody was poking around the house trying to find stuff to use later. They were all on the same side, right? Um, not exactly. A player wanted his friends to get good stuff, because he wanted help in beating the traitor. But if he knew that his friend had the Ring and the Spear and the Armor, he might've viewed him as an unbeatable threat if he turned into a demon at the end. So he wanted his friend to succeed, but not to succeed more than he succeeded.

This fixed the problem. A player couldn't direct another player's actions, because they didn't actually trust each other. If a player told another to go into the Vault, was it to get more powerful or to get saddled with something awful? *Neither player knew the answer.* Bruce figured it out: You could make a cooperative game less prone to the caller problem by *making it less cooperative.*

Then in 2008, Matt Leacock released *Pandemic* and started a revolution, and the Pandemic Problem came into its own. The bossy-pants player quite literally had the world laid out for him. I met players who swore off playing any cooperative game solely because of their bad experiences with callers in *Pandemic.* This was a shame, because *Pandemic* was awesome. But most co-op games of the day didn't seem to care. The revolution was falling apart shortly after it got going.

So, in 2011, we set about to fix it forever. My partner Rian Sand and I theorized a game for a horror world in which players would build character decks and hunt down a villain in mysterious locations. Rian made the case that in this universe, the game had to be fully cooperative, with no players wanting to work against the others. But I said something that kept us focused on sparking a new revolution:

'If we want to solve the Pandemic Problem, we have to make the players care about their characters.'

That was it. Riffing off concepts from *Arkham Horror* and Rob Daviau's *Risk Legacy* and the videogame *Diablo,* my development team—Chad Brown, Tanis O'Connor, Paul Peterson, and Gaby Weidling—and I created a new kind of persistence, making it possible to see your character grow, change, and even die. We let a player keep and remodel her character not just inside a game, but for months or even years. A character started with an array of cards: five spells, three weapons, two blessings, etc. During a scenario, characters acquired a few more of these types of cards. But at the end, they needed to return to their starting configurations, meaning that every card they gained required them to lose a card of that type. Essentially, we created the world's slowest deck-building game. And it worked.

As we shifted toward a fantasy theme, the game that would become the *Pathfinder Adventure Card Game* bore this strategy out. Players selected characters such as Harsk the dwarf ranger and Seoni the elf sorcerer, and became deeply attached to those characters. As they acquired new items and spells, they all knew that at the end, they'd communally share these new acquisitions as they rebuilt their decks.

And yet, they didn't.

Not entirely, anyway. If a player said, 'This Cure spell is better for you than me,' the subtext was, 'I would've kept this, but I've got better choices, and I want you to have it so that you can heal me when those choices don't work out.' Again, they were all on the same side, until they weren't.

Pathfinder seemed to hit a cultural zeitgeist. It sold out in four hours at its Gen Con release, and quickly jumped to the top of the Board-GameGeek rankings. Only time will tell whether we made the best game of 2013, but we definitely made the most talked-about game. I credit that popularity to players' attachment to their characters in direct contravention of the co-op spirit of the game.

So that's my solution, anyway. Someone else may come along and solve the Pandemic Problem in an entirely different way. But with *Betrayal* and *Pathfinder* and the games I've got in the hopper, I've staked my direction.

However, it hasn't come without consequence. In an interview about *Pathfinder*, I said, 'One of our goals was to solve the Pandemic Problem.' And one unidentified person took it upon himself to make sure I paid for it. On BoardGameGeek, *Pathfinder* narrowly edged out *Pandemic* for the coveted spot of 47th ranked game of all time. This is a temporary aberration, and by the time you read this, things will likely have changed.

But at that exact moment, a user created more than twenty fake accounts—so cleverly changing exactly one letter in each username to avoid detection—with two express purposes: to give the *Pathfinder* game a rating of 2 out of 10, and to give *Pandemic* a rating of 10 out of 10. He wanted to rectify this horrid slight of *Pandemic*, and show the world which game has the real problem. As you might surmise, my soul was crushed. Completely and utterly. I still haven't recovered from that dastard's vengeful act.

Y'know, it was probably Matt Leacock.

Rob
Daviau

Rob Daviau

ROB
DAVIAU

Rob Daviau

ROB DAVIAU

Rob
Daviau

ROB
DAVIAU

Ignacy about Rob:

This will be an embarrassing story about me being a jerk, but I owe it to Rob. I was a jerk and here is my penance. The Full Monty.

At Gen Con 2013 I was invited to The Dice Tower Designers Panel, along with Geoff Engelstein, Richard Launius and Rob Daviau (and a special appearance of Stephen Buonocore from Stronghold Games). Quite the company, huh?! Me? The designer of *Robinson Crusoe*. Engelstein? The designer of *Space Cadets*. Launius? *Arkham Horror* it is! And finally, Daviau. A massmarket designer who – for ages - was doing crap for Hasbro. 'What the hell is he doing here,' I thought. A Hasbro guy?! Sitting here in a jacket?! Among us geeks in t-shirts? Really? You have got to be kidding me...

That's what I was thinking when I sat there, next to Engelstein and Launius.

The first jab came quickly, right after Rob was asked to introduce himself. That's how I learned that Rob is the guy who designed *Betrayal at House on the Hill*. I have to admit, I didn't know that. Right after that came the second jab - Rob also designed *Star Wars: The Queen's Gambit*. OK, I didn't know that either. Shame on me. And then the final right hook hit me squarely in the jaw - Rob designed *Risk Legacy*. And that was me K.O.

After this quick jab, jab, right hook, I was sitting there like I had been hit by a train. But that was just the beginning. The real train was still on its way. Because after his introduction, Rob began to answer questions from Tom and the audience. And that was something truly amazing. What can I say. In only his little finger Rob holds ten times more knowledge about design, production and the board game industry in general than Engelstein and myself put together.

For years Rob had worked at Hasbro, the biggest gaming company on the planet. I was sitting there and listening. I couldn't believe how epic my underestimation had actually been. I should never judge anybody because he or she works for a company I don't entirely like. I did. Shame on me.

Last year Rob quit Hasbro and founded IronWall Games. He has new designs coming. For Gen Con 2014 he has announced *SeaFall*, a new game based on the 'legacy' concept he created for *Risk Legacy*. Believe me when I tell you – I cannot wait to have this game in my hands. I am coming back to Poland from Gen Con with *SeaFall* in my luggage. I don't care how much it will cost. I don't care how big the box is. If it means I have to leave behind clothes in the hotel, I won't think twice.

And I strongly recommend you not to think twice either!

Follow him on twitter: @robdaviaugamer
Subscribe to: http://www.robdaviau.com/

BEHOLD THE WRETCH

by Rob Daviau

Victor Frankstein, I understand you. You had the best intentions. You wanted to make something great, to push forward the bounds of science. You wanted to be remembered.

And so you are.

When you are a game designer, playing games becomes different. The mind is always turning. What is this? How is this working? Would I do the same thing? I wonder how much that component costs? Would this work better with more players? Am I winning? What's worth noting in this game?

It's even more so when you are playtesting your own games. The turns become rote. Fast. Bang bang bang. Players move their pieces quickly. Few words are spoken because you are usually testing for something specific. If you want to know if a strategy is broken, one person plays it and everyone tries to stop it. If you want to know if the end game is too long, people quickly play through the first two--thirds of the game to get to the end game. It's not bloodless, but the game is played not to be enjoyed but to be completed.

Which is why I'm horrified at Risk 2210 A.D.

This game makes everyone mad. Even me. Even when playtesting.

It's 2000 and I'm testing the game with Craig Van Ness, the co-designer. We've been tinkering with this game for a while. It is nearly done. But something isn't working. I can't remember now, but it's something that only comes out in turn 4 or 5 (it's only a 5-turn game). We get two other players and sit down to play. It's going to be bang bang bang through three turns. That's what you do with playtesting.

I idly turn to one other played, 'I'm not going to attack you here, OK, so we can get going.' He agrees. I take my turn. He takes his. Craig and the other player turn to each other.

'I guess it's them vs. us.'

'No, no, no, it's not an alliance.'

'You didn't attack each other.'

'It was just the first turn.'

'It's only a five-turn game!'

'It's playtesting!'

Craig and the other player form an alliance. They attack me mercilessly. My troops are in shambles. The playtest is in shambles. We are not going to be able to get to turn 4 or 5. I see red and stand up furiously.

'THIS IS A PLAYTEST!'

'This is Risk 2210.'

I storm off back to my office. Craig and I sit across from each other. We don't talk for the day.

We don't play the next day.

Or the one after.

Eventually we play again. But I'm afraid of this game now. It... changes people. I want it to be done and out the door.

We have created our monster.

For GenCon that year we are giving away promo cards for the game. We've put our own pictures in them and had fun with the names and powers. There are five commanders and each has a silly name. We are all Majors in the game. I think I'm Major Power and Craig is Major Death. We teasingly put one intern as Major Flöwerz. We thought the umlaut made it manly. We even threw our boss in there as a thank you for his support.

My boss comes up to me at GenCon.

'I can't believe you did that to me in the cards.' He seems... hurt.

'Uh, yeah. We thought you'd find it cool to be in the game... right? I guess we should've asked you.' I have no idea what is going on.

'You named me Major Pain. You are calling your boss a pain in the ass to everyone you give cards to.' He's not mad. He just feels like we are calling him out. He's the nicest guy I know. I feel horrible.

'No, it's not that. We just thought, you know, pain, death, destruction, power. It's thematic.'

He looks at me. He is just crushed. 'You named me Major Pain.' He walks off.

This game is evil. And we've just let it loose on the world. The monster is loose. God help us all.

A few years later some people from the office are playing the game one night at someone's house. The game has been out for a long time. Everyone there has played it before. It's nearly been forgotten by our group, brought out for old time's sake. People are drinking beers and generally behaving as you do when with friends playing games. There is trash talk and laughing and everyone is having a good time.

Until the start of turn 3.

One player declares his attack. He pushes his troops over the line. It's a calculated move that gives him a shot at the win. It also effectively cripples the other player. The defender doesn't say a single word. He stares. He stares for a while. He stands up.

He paces for a moment and then leaves the room. We hear him go into the bathroom. Not a word has been said.

We wait.

And we wait.

Too much time has passed. Nervous laughter amongst the group. What's he doing in there? Should we check on him? Is he that mad or having stomach problems?

One person gets up. He's gone from the room for a while. Finally he comes back.

'He's gone.'

'What do you mean gone?'

'Car's gone. He's gone.'

Without a word he had just left. It wasn't the bathroom at all. Confronted with the horror of what had just happened, he had simply left the game, the room, and the house, driving off into the night.

Troops were on the board. Cards left at the table. His white hot fury had driven him from the room, the game, the house.

This was the most frightening rage-quit I have ever seen. Icy cold and silent. I don't want to see it again.

This game. This Risk game. It's a monster. And I helped create it.

I am sorry.

Brad
Talton

Brad Talton

BRAD
TALTON

BRAD TALTON

BRAD TALTON

Brad
Talton

BRAD
TALTON

Ignacy about Brad:

Brad Talton has a wide range of great designs - from the real time *7-card Slugfest* to the very deep *Pixel Tactics*, from the huge *BattleCON: Devastation of Indines* to the small *NOIR: Killer vs. Inspector*. He is a young wolf, creates games one after another like crazy and he publishes them himself as the head of Level 99 Games, which is quite a successful company these days! When I look at Brad's achievements so far, I cannot but think that he is just like a boiling pot with all those great ideas just screaming to get free, to get out of his head and jump out onto our gaming tables.

I met Brad at Gen Con 2013 and I have to say – if anybody doubts whether ADHD exists, they should meet Brad. No, really, I mean it. Energy, ideas, passion and a constant lack of focus on one subject. That's my impression from Gen Con.

OK, I know, it was Gen Con. A busy time. A convention center. My impression might be a little unfair... A little.

Brad is a super guy. I am happy to publish his *Pixel Tactics* line in Poland and I hope to publish many other of his great designs here. I am also happy he is a contributor to my book. Please, check out his great designs and follow his future career closely.

Follow him on twitter: @Level99Games
Subscribe to: http://www.lvl99games.com/

GAME DESIGNS

by D. Brad Talton Jr.

Designing games has always been a very organic process for me. I'm bad at designing with an end or a mechanic in mind. Instead, I always begin with an idea—an experience that I want to create, and then alter the game until it delivers the intended experience.

In my opinion, games are not fun, people are fun, and the people you play with will determine your enjoyment (most of all dependent on whether you, yourself, are good at having fun). A game can only be successful in how well it delivers the experience we expect from it. Thus, a game must not just be well designed, but must also be up-front in the experience that it aims to deliver to the player. This experience is what the designer has to think about first and foremost when he begins a new game.

Of all the games that I've created, *BattleCON* has probably undergone the most incarnations. I could list versions that date back years, but the experience that I wanted to create in that game was always the same. Bringing it to life, first in its original form, and now again in the latest sequel, has been a sort of rite of passage for me. Each of those incarnations of the game introduced new ideas and forced me to update the game to make it more complete and fully realized.

Along the way I learned about mechanics, game theory, psychology, and player-experience. Each new concept shaped a new version of the game, often requiring a complete redesign from scratch. Always keeping your eyes open and learning, never being unwilling to take a step backward, and keeping the experience of the player at the forefront of your design are all key skills for a designer who wishes to make the best game he can create.

When searching for guidance in my designs, I always think back to the immortal words of Wolfgang Kramer (http://www.thegamesjournal.com/articles/WhatMakesaGame.shtml):

A good game will stay with us all our lives.
A good game makes us long to play it again.

How can I make a game that embodies these two principles? A game has to be an experience that the player wants, and it has to be new each time they take part in it. The game must be a test within which victory is uncertain, where the skill of the player is pitted against some balance of the opponent's skill and luck. A game must empower the player to take hold of the experience in a way that he could not in the real world. And a game must inspire the player, to make them imagine the possibilities hidden within the next play.

The best games—the ones that live for decades, like *Magic the Gathering*, *Pokemon*, and *Chess*, all embody these principles. They create a closed world in which the player can immerse himself in the experience, and which inspires him to dig ever deeper into that world.

My small hope as a designer and publisher is that I've created such games, and that I'll have the opportunity to create many more.

Adam Kałuża

Adam
Kałuża

ADAM
KAŁUŻA

ADAM KAŁUŻA

ADAM KAŁUŻA

ADAM KAŁUŻA

Adam
Kałuża

ADAM,
KAŁUŻA

Ignacy about Adam:

We have a long history with Adam. I was his first publisher. He was the first author we published. We became friends and even though Adam publishes his own games now with different publishers, we still have this very strong relationship and a very good connection. How is that possible? Adam is truly special. I can't exactly explain what it is, I don't quite understand it myself, but there is something about him I really like. A kindness, an inner calm. Serenity.

Each time I meet Adam, it's like meeting a close relative, someone I can implicitly trust, with whom I can talk about anything, with whom I have spent many great years.

He is a truly talented designer. His *K2* is an amazing game that fully deserved its nomination for Kenner Spiel des Jahres. He is the only Polish game designer with a nomination for SdJ and I have to say – I am so very happy for him. Besides this, *K2* is a great game, and Adam a great person. One of the most kind and humble people I have met in my life. I wish him all the best. I am happy he contributed to my book and I strongly encourage you to take a closer look at his designs.

FAILURE TRANSFORMED INTO SUCCESS

by Adam Kałuża

In 2006, thanks to Portal Games, my first game called *GLIK* came into being. Today, I have a dozen or so titles already released. It might look like I'm a professional author, but I don't consider myself such. On the one hand, I rather associate 'professionalism' with occupation, the full time earning of a living, and on the other, I'm still learning, seeing with each subsequent game the mistakes I made in previous designs. I still don't approach this subject with what I would consider full professionalism.

However, a dozen or so games does of course give me a certain level of experience, allowing me to talk about the subject. Therefore, dear reader, I would like to share with you what I think is most important in this profession: patience and trust.

At some point, you can come up with an idea for a game. This may be a theme that you just need to develop properly, or it could be mechanics that you will just adapt to a theme you're comfortable with. Whatever it is, the important thing is to approach it with patience. It does happen now and then, that the idea is so brilliant that after a few test games it turns into a finished work, but this is extremely rare. More often than not, a lot of work awaits you - tedious, difficult, unrewarding labor, not necessarily leading to success.

Design at this stage requires patience. When describing the process of designing a game, many authors will tell you that quite often after its release they seldom reach to the shelf for their game. The number of variants they had to test and the game elements they had to discard make their own game feel like work, and now they just want to relax. And so it is with me sometimes. However, I will return to my game with joy after some time, and I will discover it anew. But this is only after a break.

Patience is a virtue, but it's hard. It pays off though. I myself have some problems with it - I want everything fast – it is even intensified by the times we live in, but I know, this is not the right way to go about it. How do I solve this problem? I try to put the game I've been working on aside for some time, to go back to it with renewed strength and enthusiasm a bit later. This is the way of an impatient man, my way. It works in my case, but would it be useful for others? I have no idea.

While working on a game, testing, one more thing is also important - to trust yourself. If I have objections to the game, if I'm not completely happy with it, it means there's something wrong with the game. Changes have to be made. If my co-players tell me the title is good, but I still feel something is not as it should be, I check what can be changed. You should trust yourself. This also works in reverse situations. If you feel the game has potential, that it might not be perfect, but that it's getting there, then it doesn't mean you have to listen to all the testers' opinions, their 'good advice'. You have to be the author, you decide, and you also suffer the consequences of such decisions.

Frankly, I don't know which is easier for me, I think the latter. Postponing a game that might be released, convincing the publisher it's not time yet, even though he's ready to move forward with publication, is very difficult. I know what I'm talking about, as I've been in such a situation. It has also happened that I had to listen to the testers - in fact, it happens with almost every game. I listened, but did not always react. I still listen, but I don't always do as they wish. I try to trust my experience. Does it always work? No. For example, ages ago *Ski Jumping* was published. One of the testers said it would be better if the scoring changed from the classical ski jumping scoring to a simpler scoring method, based on a scale of one to ten. And I didn't listen, when I should have.

From among my games so far the greatest success has of course been *K2*. A nomination for Spiel des Jahres is something I had never dreamed of. But before it happened, the game was put aside in accordance with the patience principle and, in accordance with the trust principle, I listened to my convictions, but also to the testers, which resulted in further changes. There's quite a lot to read about this game on the web, as I've presented a fairly accurate description of its creation there, but I haven't written about yet another very important experience connected to this game. Before *K2* was accepted and released by REBEL.pl, four other publishers saw the game. Not all at the same design stage, but they had the chance to get to know the game and publish it. Still, they rejected it, which hurt really badly, as I was convinced it was a good game. This, however, was a very important lesson for me. It was a defeat that turned into a success, both for me and for the publisher who decided to take a risk on me and my game.

Patience and trust, self-confidence - these are very important features in my opinion. If you seriously plan to try your hand at game design, I'm sure you'll need them, and that's what I wish you.

IGNACY TRZEWICZEK

Well, Vlaada is the guy on the left. On the right is Michiel Hendriks, the designer of *Legacy: The Testament of Duke de Crecy* and the owner of this photo (thanks, Michiel!).

Ignacy about Vlaada:

In this book you will find articles that tell the story of me testing *Robinson Crusoe* with Vlaada. What you may not know is the fact that he has a great history in both RPG game and computer game design. Before he became a world famous board game designer he was very successful in those two other design areas. A very talented guy.

I first met Vlaada in Essen 2008. We decided with CGE to have our booths next to each other because our designs have a common philosophy – a euro mechanism blended with an ameritrash style. CGE has *Galaxy Trucker*, Portal Games has *Neuroshima Hex*, CGE has *Through the Ages*, we have *Stronghold*, they have *Dungeon Petz*, we have *Legacy*. These are all super thematic eurogames.

For many visitors it was always a *must-take-route* – find hall 4 and visit the CGE and Portal Games booths. It worked perfectly.

Because of his education, Vlaada works very differently from me. As Petr Murmak from CGE once told me, Vlaada often creates a software version of his prototypes and then tests them with a computer, using technology to make his games well balanced. Before he shows it to people, he wants it to be as good as possible – and that is why he uses a computer. I find it fascinating that we both aim to create 'euro-trash', but we do work in totally different ways. For me sending an email is just about the most I can do with a computer.

Vlaada is one of the best designers out there. He has two great games in the Top 10 at BGG and three more great games in the Top 100. I personally love *Galaxy Trucker*, which I find pure fun. And you know, games should be fun, right?

WHEN A GAME TELLS A STORY

by Vlaada Chvatil

Elsewhere in this book, Ignacy writes about our experience with an early version of *Robinson Crusoe: Adventure on the Cursed Island*. Funny reading, I said to myself, but hell - how did Ignacy come to the conclusion that I do not like John McClane? Bruce Willis is one of my favorite actors and John McClane is my favorite action hero. (No, sorry, I do not want to discuss the latest Die Hard sequels. :) I would definitely love to see a hero that acts like John McClane in a game.

But then I realized that Ignacy didn't want to have McClane-like characters in his game. He expected us, the players, to feel and perform like John McClane when the game screws us. Well, that didn't work. Bad rolls or bad cards are not like pain and misery. You do not overcome them with a strong will. Nor even by smarter play - gamers usually do their best at a game even if not in a bad situation. And when the bad luck in a game has a much bigger impact than any of the options the game offers you, you do not feel like John McClane. You feel like Hans Gruber, losing one man after another, while the game engine heads to the inevitable Yippee ki-yay.

To have John McClane as a character in a game, I would adjust the game mechanics. When wounded, he might have lower stats, but

251

IGNACY TRZEWICZEK

I would, for example, give him more cards or better dice to roll to simulate his improvement in performance when he is in trouble. And then, I would love to watch him solve the most hopeless situations.

Anyway, this led me to more thoughts about how we can view a game's theme and story. Let me share a few of them.

For many players, strong theme equals strong immersion - you feel a connection with your character, you feel like him or her, you make decisions the way he or she would and experience the story from his or her perspective. That's great of course, and I love to identify with a story hero... but honestly, board games are not the strongest medium for this. A good book or movie offers this more efficiently. If I want to immerse myself actively in a story, I can play a good videogame. If I want to add a social aspect to that, I can LARP or play a pen-and-paper RPG. But board games usually do not offer both good immersion and good gameplay.

There is a reason for that - the game mechanics themselves. To achieve real immersion, you need the player to forget about mechanics and approach the game situations intuitively, as if they were real. But in a classic board game, the mechanics are there, and the players see them and have to work with them, as there is no CPU or Game Master to do it for them.

This may be one of the reasons why dice rolling is evergreen in combat games. Emotionally, tossing a bunch of dice does not feel so different from thrusting forward recklessly with a sword or axe. The mechanics are there, but players accept them as a direct analogy to the game world actions. It works as long as you keep it simple - a better weapon means more or better dice; to defeat a bigger monster, you need to roll better. Many other factors that would affect the chance of success are ignored and just replaced by the randomness of the roll.

When you want to make it more interesting from a gameplay point-of-view, you start losing that immersion. When you add various modifiers, bonuses, reroll options and other special abilities, you make the player think differently from his hero. Is it better to add a die to your roll, to improve your chance from hitting at 4+ to 3+, or to have a chance to make one reroll? That's sure not the way your warrior is thinking.

We are still deep in the territory of what is called American style gaming, and yet we are slowly starting to lose the immersion in favor of more interesting gameplay. As the game design evolves, the designers are introducing more and more mechanics that are interesting from a gameplay point of view, but not well connected to reality. For example, hand management is a very interesting mechanic, but how to explain that you can perform only the actions you have cards for? Well, you may say your hero is restricted by various random conditions he or she can't affect. But when you are thinking about how to get a particular card into your hand or whether to discard some cards to be able to draw better ones or how to thin your deck in a deckbuilding game, then your way of thinking and the point-of-view of your character have definitely parted.

I have to admit, as a player, I prefer elegant and interesting mechanics, too. In fact, I do not want the game to hide the mechanics from me. Although I can play tons of videogames that go for immersion on my computer or iPad, I spend much more time playing board game implementations or games with interesting mechanics on these devices.

But at the same time, I love it when a board game tells a strong story. This does not contradict with what I have said. The difference is in the perspective from which you view that story.

I do not mind that I am not living the story personally. I can watch my hero live it (or my nation, or corporation, or alien race, or family, or whatever I am in control of). If the game is good and thematic, the story it creates is interesting, atmospheric, emotional, and my hero has a strong role in that story. I am at his side, I am cheering him on, I am happy if he is doing well and sad when he is failing, but I am perfectly okay with the fact that I am not him. I can (and love to) imagine what he feels and how he sees the situation, I feel the mood of his game world, but at the same time, I am aware of all the mechanics he does not see. If I play the game well, my actions help him to achieve his goals in the game world. Interesting game situations may translate into important decisions in the game world, brilliant gameplay actions into unexpected plot twists, and generally, the progress of my character is a nice reward for my good game play. My thinking does not have to be realistic in the given situation if the results it leads to are believable and thrilling.

By the way, this is also how I try to develop my own games. I love to think about interesting mechanics, but I always want them to be related to the game world. I am aware for many players it may be a reason to dislike my games: those who require immersion may not like the heavier mechanics that distract them, and those who do not care about story at all may dislike the details that are here for a rich story. But I am lucky that there are enough players with similar tastes around the world, so I can create the games the way I like them.

For me, a game succeeds at telling a good story when you can write down the session as an interesting tale, ideally in a way that an unsuspecting person would hardly recognize as a session report, but the player who knows the game well can reconstruct the game flow from it. I love such games (and such session reports, by the way :). It was a pleasure to see that Robinson Crusoe turned out to be one of these games!

Iraklis Iraklis IRAKLIS IRAKLIS Iraklis IRAKLIS

Ignacy about Iraklis.

Iraklis talks a lot. Really. I mean, his mouth never shuts up. He talks and talks. And at the same time he works, all the time. He never stops. He is new to our hobby, and yet in the past few months he has already published two games (*Byzantio* and *Gears & Piston*), managed dozens of successful Kickstarter campaigns, organized Boardgametravel holidays and now he is publishing other games and organizing another Boardgametravel event, and...

He works a lot. And he talks a lot. And he is new.

I was lucky to have Iraklis managing my campaign. He did a great job and the campaign was a tremendous success. I met him in person at Essen 2013 for the first time and I have to say – he talks a lot. But he also works a lot. And he is new. So keep an eye on him, please.

Follow him on twitter: @LudiCreations
Subscribe to: http://ludicreations.com/
and http://boardgametravel.com/

KICKSTARTER CAMPAIGNS
THAT TELL STORIES

by Iraklis, LudiCreations

Fire up your nearest internet-machine. Go to Kickstarter.com. Look at a project, any project. It doesn't even have to be a board game project. You'll see sweat, and tears, and effort, and passion and... and.. and... stories.

You will see a creator fighting with his inner self, trying to create something that will be the next Big Thing. You will see a writer, talented as heck, struggling with a few words on a campaign page. You will see a photographer, trying to figure out which few pictures to show. You will see a board game designer, compromising on how much of that heavy backstabbing game he can explain before he loses you to a flashlight-axe-wallet project, or to cat videos.

Stories. Each campaign page tells a story. There are real people behind each one, even the big 'corporate' ones. Some backers only see numbers – goals, backers, pledge levels. I can tell you, there is a reason for each one. Multiple reasons. Some creators have spent 3 days thinking about how to set that single pledge reward level. Some should have.

Ignacy is no fool. He's busy, and he's overworked, but no fool. He knows what Kickstarter does – or rather, he knows what it could do. I tell him, man, it's work – it's not easy. OK, he knows. Good. So, Ignacy, what do you want to kickstart? Something small. Fine, so what, a minigame? An expansion? No, a book. A what?

Yes, I know the blog, I read it too.

[30 May 13 15:57:49] - Iraklis -: I am just worried.

[30 May 13 15:58:29] - Iraklis -: Because I know how to sell the games, and the game idea. When people are pledging, they are pledging for the book. Will there be any extras?

[30 May 13 15:58:47] - Iraklis -: What I am basically trying to say, is that I am not sure this will be a succesful project.

[30 May 13 15:59:00] - Iraklis -: And I mean that literally.

[30 May 13 15:59:05] - Iraklis -: That I am not sure.

[30 May 13 15:59:24] - Iraklis -: I am not saying that it will not, I am just saying that I would like to know more.

[30 May 13 15:59:47] - Iraklis -: It's hard to express 'I am not sure' in a non-negative tone :)

[30 May 13 16:03:08] Ignacy Trzewiczek: I don't know it too. I see the problem - would anybody be interested in paying cash for something that he already read on the blog. I would say: No :)

But on the other hand, if I do it right, I mean - add some new txt, add some cool photos etc, ask subscribers that it is a nice way to say: 'Thank you' for my work on the blog... Perhaps I will find 50 or 70 people who will say: 'OK, I read your post every single wednesday. I like them. Here is my 10$ for you'

Printing a book is far less expensive than boardgame, so I will be sucesfull if I gather 1000 usd or something like that.

There it is, ladies and gentlemen. When we were saying during the campaign that we would be happy, really happy with $1000, we meant it. I was doubtful I could help Ignacy raise even that much.

I mean, raising money for a game is hard enough. And it takes time. And it takes people. More than just the designer, the publisher and the backers. Someone needs to make the video. Someone needs to make the voiceover for the video. Someone needs to write the script for the voiceover for the video. Someone needs to proofread the script for the voiceover for the video. And so on. And this is just for one part of the whole thing.

For every campaign you see, it is like any good story – there are characters, heroes (and sometimes villains), there is a plot, there is a beginning, a middle and an end. People think that launching a campaign is a beginning – far from it – it is, in itself, the end of a very stressful period. When I hit 'Launch', that's when I can actually breathe – done. Oh wait, not done, shit. First comments in. First dollars, too. Time to worry again.

Spend any more than 5 minutes discussing crowdfunding, and you'll have someone telling you about the 'spirit of Kickstarter'. Bullshit. There's no such thing. There's only dollars.

'Might is right' - goes one adage. 'Right, as the world goes, is only in question between equals in power, while the strong do what they can and the weak suffer what they must,' (google it) goes another – it doesn't matter how you think Kickstarter should be used. It doesn't matter what you think the point of crowdfunding is. It doesn't even matter if you 'vote with your dollars'. This is the crowd baby, welcome to a brave new world.

If a big publisher uses Kickstarter as a glorified pre-order system, and Kickstarter approves the campaign, it's on. It's right. It's good. Kosher. Halal. Supercalifragilisticexpialidocious. Post all the comments you want, they'll still do it. Haters gonna hate, backers gonna back. And you know what? I don't mind. In fact, I kinda like it.

Let's assume that yes, it does take money away from my campaigns. Sure, I'm a poor, defenseless, small publisher with nary a big-name designer in my range. So what am I to do? Curl up and click 'Cancel Campaign'? No. I'm going to put my best product out there, and hope people love it. Not like it, love it. The more the campaign funds in a time someone's million-dollar minis campaign is up, the sweeter that 'Congratulations! Your project was successfully funded' email.

But you see, I don't think that it takes money away from my campaigns. Sure, maybe a bit. Not enough to matter. Because I'm in this for the long haul. I know I'll never compete with the big boys in equal terms. I'll be small fry no matter if it's on Kickstarter, or off it. At least here I get a shot. There's no 4-5 distributor-gatekeepers. There's 4000-5000. And you know what? The more the big boys use this, the more backers there are. The more legitimacy the system has.

So don't worry about what the 'spirit of Kickstarter' is – especially if you don't run campaigns – just back the games you love – yes, love. And, although I've never heard this from a creator, if you run campaigns, don't worry about the 'big ones', and don't go looking for excuses (I hate excuses). You'll never change how this works – it's been like this long before Kickstarter came along. Make a better product, run a better campaign, let people fall in love with what you're offering.

Love. Yeah, I said love. This is what makes people buy flowers, get on one knee, and spew stereotypes (see what I did there?). There's a lot of love on Kickstarter. Some of it doomed love, some giving way to hate. Sometimes it works out, other times you want to break up. Once or twice it brings entitlement, bitterness, downright ugly trolling. But, in the end, you know – it's worth it.

Seeing someone play your game, your product, your passion is something else. Even if they hate it – it doesn't matter – you made this happen, this moment, this experience. You are no longer just a consumer, you are a creator. When you die – and you will – you will leave this behind. A product of our times, our culture.

Even the campaign itself is that, a product. And there's a story – a story about someone making something – or trying to, anyway. There's sleepless nights, and annoyed significant others. There's changes on the illustrations. There's running through the rain at Essen to sit down with 8 Polish people and launch a campaign during Spiel. There's non-stop, uncompromising, take-no-prisoners drive and determination. And there's not getting to play all that many board games these days.

But you know what, if I am to do that, I am damn glad and proud to be making board games.

Merry Merry

MERRY

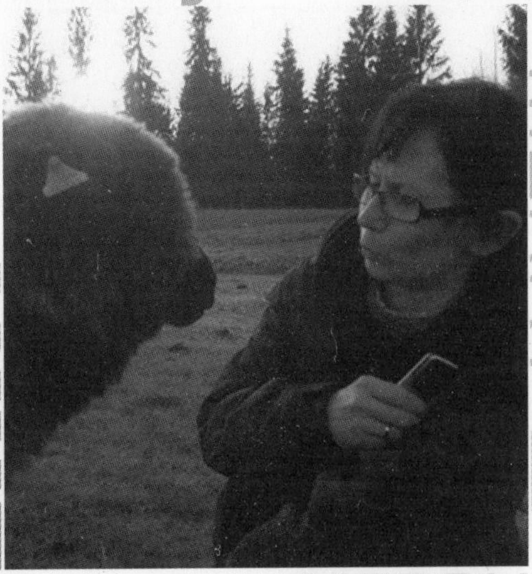

MERRY

MERRY

Merry

MERRY

Ignacy about Merry:
Without Merry there would be nothing. I would not design games.
I would not attend cons. I would not write a blog.

All I do, I do because of her. She gives me power, fuels my passion
and encourages me to always try harder.

So my friends, I do ask you to buy her a beer or a snack when you
meet her at a convention.

She is our precious! She keeps me alive. She keeps me focused.

We do all want her to succeed with this as long as possible.

Right?

EPILOGUE

by Merry

After the many articles that he has written on BGG, you already know a lot about Ignacy. You know he is funny. You know he loves his job. You know how he feels about his games. You know a lot. But maybe there is something you do not know. Let's call it a different perspective. I am more than happy to share it with you.

Ignacy is 190cm tall and he is very, very slim. I mean VERY. He loves tea. And biscuits. Many years ago his friends gave him the nickname, 'Biscuit'. Personally I think because he is as thin as a biscuit, not because he loves biscuits.

Ignacy loves football. He loves playing football. Every Monday he plays and comes back late at night and says, 'I am too old to play, too old. Next Monday I will not play.' He has been saying this for many years now.

Ignacy loves silence. Especially when I want to listen to my music. We do not like the same kind of music. He likes soul and blues, and many soppy romantic songs.

Ignacy loves movies. He has a large movie collection. But he does not have time enough to watch them all. So every time he buys a new movie, he says, 'This weekend we are going to watch it!'

It never happens.

Ignacy is afraid of dogs, but he also lives with four dogs. Our dogs know that when Ignacy is at home alone, they can do whatever they want. And that is exactly what they do.

Ignacy has a special skill. He destroys every computer that he uses. I have my own computer and believe me, Ignacy is banned from even going near it. Really. Forever.

Ignacy is a perfectionist. When he does something it has to be perfect. But this applies only to games.

Ignacy is afraid of food. He does not eat anything he does not know. He loves tomato soup and some meat dishes. That's all. Until five years ago he didn't want to eat fish because, in his opinion, they have strange names.

Ignacy hates water, I mean lakes, the seaside, etc. He hates airplanes, ships and everything you can use to travel because he hates travelling.

He hates when I watch The Big Bang Theory and laugh. He knows why I laugh.

Ignacy is very romantic. But only in his RPG. And sarcastic. But only in real life. And he loves to be at home.

And finally...

'The Most Beautiful Girl (in the Room)' by Flight of the Conchords is a song he still sings to me.

boardgames
that tell
stories.com

boardgames that
tell stories.com

BOARDGAMES
THAT TELL
STORIES.COM

FOLLOW ME!

HTTP://BOARDGAMESTHATTELLSTORIES.COM @trzewik